Mastering
Adobe Illustrator 2024

Your Ultimate Toolkit for Crafting Seamless Arts, Visual Innovations and Digital Illustrations from Beginner to Pro

McBunny Albert

TABLE OF CONTENTS

INTRODUCTION

Adobe Illustrator is a popular tool for creating and editing digital images with smooth lines and curves, known as vector graphics. This book is a helpful book that explains how to use the latest version of this software. It is written for both beginners and advanced users, and aims to improve their skills in creating illustrations and designs. "Adobe Illustrator 2024" is a comprehensive guidebook that explores the features of the newest version of Adobe Illustrator. The book is written for those who want to be experts in graphic design and Adobe software, making it easy for anyone to learn and make the most of this powerful program.

Features of the book:

- **Easy-to-use Interface:** The book starts by explaining the different parts of Adobe Illustrator, like the menus and tools, so readers can navigate the software more easily.
- If you're new to Adobe Illustrator, this book covers the basic ideas behind vector graphics, like layers, shapes, and paths. This information is important for creating more complex artwork.
- **Detailed Tools and Techniques:** The book goes into depth about the many tools and techniques available in Adobe Illustrator. You'll learn how to use the drawing tools, shape manipulation, typography, color schemes, and blending options. You are provided with clear instructions and examples to guide you through each step.
- **Advanced Techniques:** As you become more familiar with the software, the book covers more advanced techniques such as creating custom brushes, using the pen tool effectively, working with gradients and meshes, and applying 3D effects to make your illustrations look more realistic.
- **Efficient Workflow:** "Adobe Illustrator 2024" also provides tips to work more efficiently. You'll learn shortcuts, how to set up artboards for different devices, automate repetitive tasks, and collaborate with other Adobe Creative Cloud apps.
- **Real-life Examples and Projects:** Throughout the book, you'll find real-life examples and engaging projects to apply what you've learned. These projects challenge you to use your creativity and provide a hands-on learning experience.
- **Stay Up-to-date:** Since this book focuses on Adobe Illustrator 2024, it includes information on any changes and new features in the software. You'll learn about

updates to the user interface, new tools, enhancements, and additional capabilities.

As you go through the pages of this book, you'll find out that this is a helpful resource for mastering Adobe Illustrator. With its easy-to-understand language, step-by-step instructions, and practical examples, the book will improve your skills using the latest version of this powerful design software. Whether you're a beginner or more experienced, this book will help you make the most of Adobe Illustrator.

OVERVIEW

Each chapter of this book is designed to help you learn and master Adobe Illustrator step by step. Here's a sneak peek at what you would get in this book:

CHAPTER 1: WHAT'S NEW IN ADOBE ILLUSTRATOR 2024 - You will find out about the latest updates and features in the newest version of Adobe Illustrator.

CHAPTER 2: GETTING STARTED - This chapter will cover the basics of starting with Adobe Illustrator, including what it is, how it works and understanding the interface.

CHAPTER 3: GETTING FAMILIAR WITH THE WORK AREA - You will become familiar with the different parts of the Adobe Illustrator work area, like the creating a new document, configuring your workspace, and panels.

CHAPTER 4: GETTING TO KNOW ALL ADOBE ILLUSTRATOR TOOLS - This chapter will explain all the tools available in Adobe Illustrator and how to use them effectively.

CHAPTER 5: CREATING A GREAT-LOOKING LOGO DESIGN - You will learn how to make an attractive logo design using different techniques in Adobe Illustrator.

CHAPTER 6: HOW TO MANAGE AND WORK WITH ARTBOARDS - This chapter will teach you how to handle and work with multiple artboards in Adobe Illustrator.

CHAPTER 7: WORKING WITH LAYERS - You will learn how to organize and work with layers to manage your artwork efficiently in Adobe Illustrator.

CHAPTER 8: WORKING WITH COLORS - This chapter will cover different color modes, creating color swatches, and using color effectively in Adobe Illustrator.

CHAPTER 9: WORKING WITH TEXT - You will learn how to add and format text in Adobe Illustrator, including using text tools and effects.

CHAPTER 10: HOW TO EDIT ILLUSTRATOR TEMPLATE - This chapter will guide you on how to edit and customize Illustrator templates to fit your designs.

CHAPTER 11: WORKING WITH GRADIENTS, PATTERNS, and BLENDS - You will explore creating and using gradients, patterns, and blends to enhance your designs.

CHAPTER 12: INSTALLING AND APPLYING BRUSHES - This chapter will teach you how to install and use different brushes in Adobe Illustrator.

CHAPTER 13: APPLYING EFFECTS - You will learn how to add various effects to your artwork in Adobe Illustrator, such as shadows, 3D effects, and distortions.

CHAPTER 14: GOING PRO WITH ILLUSTRATOR - This chapter will provide advanced tips and techniques for professional graphic designers using Adobe Illustrator.

CHAPTER 15: DESIGN A T-SHIRT TEMPLATE - You will learn how to design a t-shirt template using Adobe Illustrator, including creating custom graphics and applying them to a template.

CHAPTER 16: WORKING WITH IMAGES - This chapter will cover importing, editing, and manipulating images in Adobe Illustrator.

CHAPTER 17: MASKING IN ADOBE ILLUSTRATOR - You will learn how to use masks to crop and blend elements in Adobe Illustrator.

CHAPTER 18: SAVING AND SHARING YOUR CREATIONS - This chapter will guide you on how to save and export your Illustrator artwork in different formats and share them with others.

CHAPTER 19: ILLUSTRATOR SHORTCUTS YOU MUST KNOW - You will discover essential keyboard shortcuts to improve your workflow and efficiency in Adobe Illustrator.

CHAPTER 20: ILLUSTRATOR SECRETS GRAPHIC DESIGNERS MUST KNOW - This final chapter will reveal advanced secrets and tips for experienced graphic designers using Adobe Illustrator.

CHAPTER 1

WHAT'S NEW IN ADOBE ILLUSTRATOR 2024

In this introductory chapter, we are going to show you all the new features that were just added in the Adobe Illustrator 2024 update and take you through how to use them.

Text to Vector Graphic

First, we have the highly anticipated Text to Vector Graphics. To open this, go up to "Window" and select "Text to Vector Graphics."

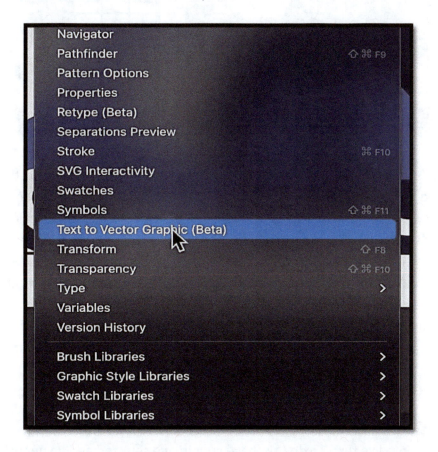

You can then select the shape tool and draw out the area where you want your graphic to be. In the panel on the right, you can select the type of graphic you want, and you can use the eyedropper to sample the graphic style that you want.

If you sample your illustration here, it will try to match its style. Then simply type in what you want to create, hit "Generate," and it's going to give you a few options to choose from. Now you can see that this is a full vector graphic that you can scale and move around. Let's try to create a background scene for an image. We are going to draw our shape over the artboard and send it to the back. Then change the type to be seen, and we're going to type our text, for this illustration we'll say "airport." Don't forget to sample your image. Once we've done that, we'll hit "Generate," and this brings up a few results here. As you can see, they're not perfect, but it's a start and certainly helpful when you want to quickly test a concept. It does a pretty good job of creating clean vector art.

Retype tool

Next, we have the new Retype tool that can identify fonts from an image and let you convert them into live text. To do this, have your image selected and go up to "Type" and down to "Retype."

This will then analyze and highlight text areas in your image. Select the area that you want to identify, and it will provide you with a list of fonts that will match it. You can filter these fonts by Web fonts and System fonts.

Once you've found a font that you like, you can download it straight from Adobe by selecting the cloud icon here. Once it's downloaded, double-click the text on your image to convert it to live text. Then, if you hit "Exit," you can now type directly onto the image and adjust it to where you want. This will be great for customizing images and prototyping designs.

Share for Review

Next is the new Share for Review tool that makes collaborating and receiving feedback from clients easy. You can even share with those who don't have a Creative Cloud account. To do this, simply click the "Share" button in the right-hand corner, add your file name, adjust access, and click "Create Link."

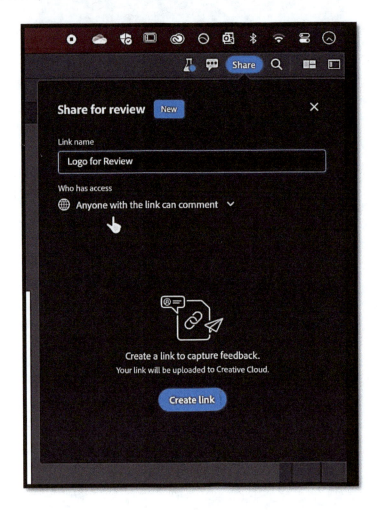

Within the Share for Review panel, you have the flexibility to adjust access settings, and even add a password by clicking "More Options" then "Link Settings." Hit the toggle here, and now you can set your password. To make sure they're seeing the latest designs, hit "Update Content," then copy the link to share.

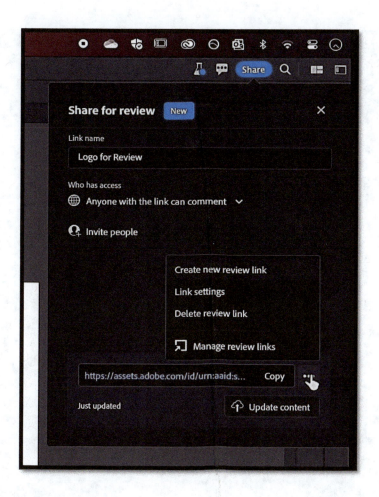

Recipients with the link can access it with the password you created. Then, they can add any comments to the design. They can even add pins to comment on certain areas or mark out changes with the pen tool and attach comments to the marking. All comments appear live in your design file, where you can reply and make any necessary changes. If you don't have the comments window showing, you can select it by going to "Window" and then "Comments."

Once a change has been made, you can resolve the comment by clicking the message icon here, so you can track what changes you've made. Live comments can be toggled on and off by selecting the Live icon at the bottom, and you can also filter comments by reviewer, time, status, and any unread comments. Once you're finished making changes, go back to "Share" and click "Update Content." This amazing new tool is going to save you time and streamline the review process.

The New Contextual Taskbar

Next, we have the new contextual taskbar that displays the most relevant actions in your workflow. For example, if you select a grouped object, it's going to come up with options like recolor, ungroup, repeat object, duplicate object, and lock. When selecting text, you can change the font, font size, area type, and outline the text.

10

This bar might get a little bit annoying as it follows you around, so you can simply move it out of the way, and it's going to lock to the new position. To reset this, select "More Options" and go to "Reset bar position."

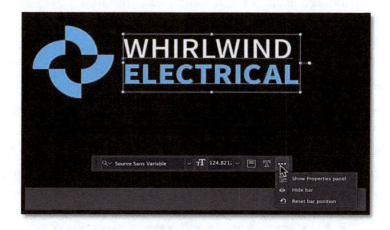

You can also hide the bar, which is going to remove it. To bring the contextual taskbar back, simply go up to "Window" and select "Contextual Taskbar."

The New Mockup Tool

Next, we have the new mockup tool, which allows you to mock up your designs onto any image. You can even explore the new Mockup library, which allows you to mock up your designs in just one click. The first thing you need to do is find an image of your mockup. Paste your image into Illustrator and then add your artwork. For instance, let's say you want to use a logo that needs to be a vector. You can position it roughly to where you want it in your image. Then select both the image and the artwork, and in the menu, go to "Object," "Mockup" and "Make."

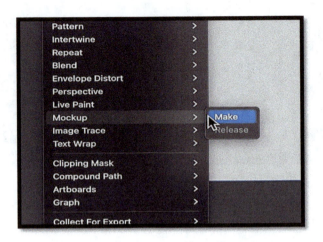

You can now drag your logo around the file and position it in the best place. You can see it recognizes the shape of your mockup and distorts your artwork to match. You can play around with your blend modes under "Transparency" to create a more realistic result. If you have an Adobe Stock account, you can also choose from a library of pre-designed mockup templates for various projects, from branding graphics to digital devices, saving you a ton of time when creating presentations for clients. To do this, make sure you have the mockup window active by selecting "Window," "Mockup" in your top menu. Now, with your artwork selected, click the mockup button here. This will apply the artwork to all the mockup templates. Select "Edit on Canvas," and you can make changes by double-clicking your design and adjusting the frame.

The Smooth Tool

Last but not least is the Smooth Tool. To illustrate this, we're going to draw a wonky line. With your line selected, go up to "Object," "Path" then "Smooth."

This is going to open up a slider here, where you can adjust the smoothness of your line. There's also the "Auto Smooth" button, but you might prefer to do it manually as it seems to be more effective.

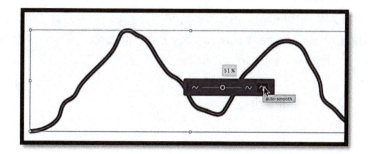

Review Questions

1. What are the key features and updates introduced in the latest version of Adobe Illustrator that enhance the user experience?
2. How do the new updates in Adobe Illustrator 2024 improve workflow efficiency and productivity for graphic designers?
3. Provide examples of specific tasks or processes that have been made easier or more efficient with the new features introduced in Adobe Illustrator 2024.

CHAPTER 2
GETTING STARTED

If you want to create printables, presentations, SVGs, mockups, and more, then Adobe Illustrator is a great program to get to know. We are going to be starting with the basic workspace in this chapter and then working our way through some lessons that will teach you how to use Adobe Illustrator to make your own files. In this chapter, we're going to talk a little bit about why Adobe Illustrator is so good for creating these files and then we're going to walk through the workspace. We'll start by talking about what Illustrator is great at, what it's mediocre at but still gets used for and what it's not good at, when you should look at some of the other products to go and use then we will show you how to open it up, create a new file, and look at all the parts of Illustrator.

We'll also talk about a few of the tools that you're going to need to know, and then as we proceed we will go into more depth on certain features and tools. Before we get started, we want you to know that Adobe Illustrator can be intimidating, but if you give yourself the space and time to learn, it is a robust program that will allow you to create beautiful designs that can be cut natively. Some designers are primarily self-taught in Illustrator, they started using it more and that is how they became pros, which is great news for you because that means that you also do not need a fancy graphic design education to be able to use Illustrator. It also means that there are so many ways to do all the processes, it is a process of figuring out what works best for you.

 Are you ready?

What is Adobe Illustrator?

Illustrator is a vector drawing software, which despite its name, is primarily used for graphic design.

What is a vector? Well, in design, a vector is an image that can be scaled to infinity without losing quality. It's the opposite of a bitmap image, like a photo, which is made out of pixels and has a set resolution. But then, you can still use bitmap images inside Illustrator, it's just not what it's best at.

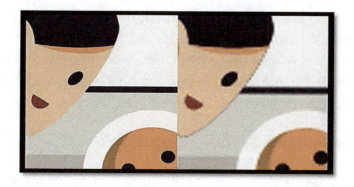

Adobe Illustrator as a vector design software

Before we dive in with the parts of our workspace, let's talk about how Adobe Illustrator is vector design software. This means that Illustrator works in points, which we're going to call anchor points, and in lines called paths. This, instead of pixels, like Photoshop might work with photos, JPEGs, PNGs, and those sorts of files. You may hear those also referred to as raster images or bitmap images. The wonderful thing about vectors is that they can be resized to any size you need them to be. You can make them very small or very large and they never lose any resolution or quality.

Vector vs. pixels

From our image below, over here on the left we have a vector Popsicle, and then over here on the right we have a pixel Popsicle.

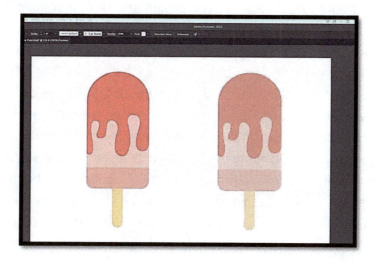

Now obviously you can see here on the right that this is already pixelated, but if we go over here to the left and zoom in, we can see that no matter how far we zoom in, it doesn't get pixelated at all. It's similar to how a lot of fonts work. You can enlarge a font and put it on a billboard and it will look the same as if you print it out on your home printer and that's because fonts are vector-based, or at least most fonts are vector-based.

Why is a vector-based system important?

Why is this vector-based system important? Because if you think about how a cutting machine works, it cuts in lines and it turns at points, which is exactly how a vector file is built. If you try to upload a bitmap pixel image to Cricut Design Space, for example, it will try to turn it into a print and then cut the image. It'll cut around the edge but it won't have any of the details. However, if you upload a vector image like an SVG, your Cricut will be able to cut your image just fine.

What you can do with Illustrator

Adobe Illustrator is good for things like illustration and drawing perfect logo design, branding, illustrators, perfect Flyers, posters, stationary, stickers, icons, fashion, patent making and sign writing.

What you shouldn't do with Illustrator

Now have an idea of what Illustrator is used for by lots of people, you should also know that it's probably not the right tool for Web design and UI design mainly because there are there are products like Figo, XD or Envision Studio and lots of other products that are more focused on doing that. You can design them an Illustrator but adding all the interactivity can't be done here so it's better to go to those tools. The other thing that it's not good at is newsletters, magazines and books. Recall that earlier on we said it's good for newsletters, what we mean is newsletters that are really small; the problem with it is Illustrator is designed to do illustration amazingly quickly and beautifully which is great but as soon as you add lots of volume to it like four or eight pages it starts struggling and slowing down especially if you start throwing in lots of big high quality Images and that is where something like Adobe InDesign comes in. It does a little bit of what Illustrator does but it allows you to do multiple pages. You can open a 300-page document and InDesign will work perfectly fine but with Illustrator, it becomes extremely slow and annoying so doing a few pages is fine in Illustrator but for lots of pages you need to move to InDesign. The other big thing that's in the group of Illustrator, especially if you're a designer or a book publisher, is Photoshop. Photoshop is for retouching images. With Illustrator you can do tiny changes, you can do tweaks and color shifts but you can't mask anything, you can't cut anybody out since that is Photoshop's job. So any sort of photo manipulation, masking and cutting gets done in Photoshop. Illustrator does all the illustration and creates lots of little elements, icons, buttons, titles and drawings and then InDesign is over here for if it gets published in a larger book.

The Welcome Screen

When you first open Illustrator you'll be greeted with the home screen. There are a few presets to choose from, a list of recently opened files, and what's most important: the "New file" button.

Upon clicking it, a menu will pop up with some settings you can customize for your new file, like size, measurement unit, how many artboards you want, and some advanced options like Color Mode.

A Quick Tip: Use RGB for anything digital, and CMYK for anything that'll be printed.

The workspace

After setting everything up and clicking the "Create" button, you'll reach the most important part of the program, which is the workspace. Everything (every tool, menu, and panel) you see on the screen can be customized and moved around.

There are also different workspace presets for different workflows, which you can access in the top right corner of Illustrator. For now, let's select the Essential Classics preset, just so we're both on the same page and also because this preset is very good for starters.

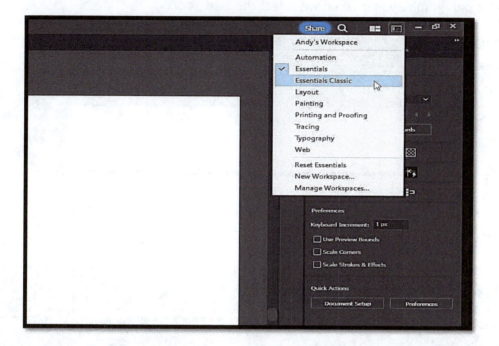

The workspace in Illustrator can be separated into different parts, and knowing them will help you understand the software. On the very top, we have the **Header**. Here, you'll find all the menus. A lot of things in Illustrator can be done in several different ways, but more often than not, you can find what you're looking for in the menus.

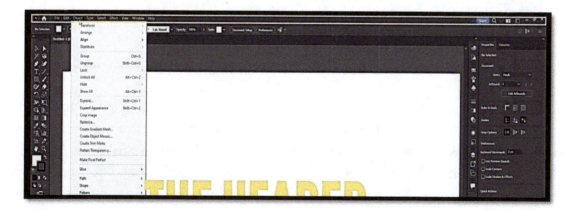

Down below we have the **Control Bar**. It is one of the most helpful elements of the workspace because it is context-based - meaning its contents will change depending on the object or the tool you have selected. For example, you'll notice how new options like font and paragraph appear when we select the Text Tool.

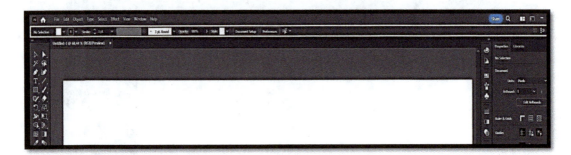

Below the Control Bar, we have the **Document Tabs**. Each tab is a different file you have opened.

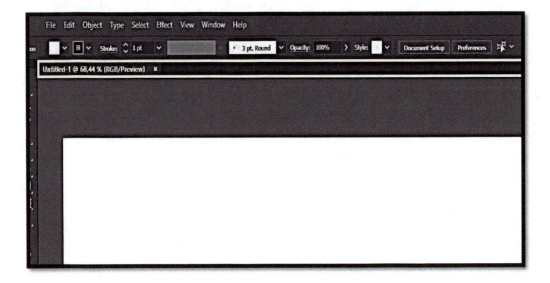

On the left side, we have the **Toolbar**, which contains all the tools in Illustrator. If you hover the mouse over a tool, Illustrator will show the tool name, its shortcut, and a small video explaining what the tool does. If a tool has a small arrow on the corner, you can click it and hold it to open up similar tools, for example, clicking and holding on the Rectangle Tool opens a menu containing similar tools like the Ellipse Tool and the Polygon Tool.

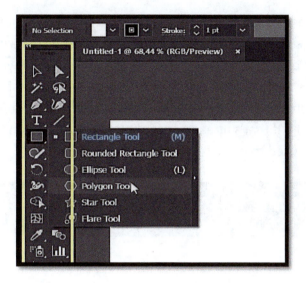

On the right side, we have the **panels**. Illustrator has several different panels and they're all used to perform different actions, like aligning objects, customizing gradients, and combining shapes. They can all be opened through the Window menu and they are more like a complement to the Toolbar. Panels can be expanded or collapsed using the arrow symbol on the top right corner.

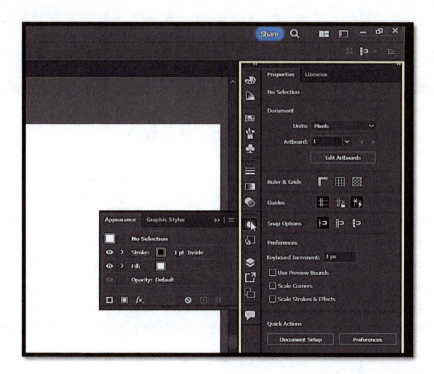

On the bottom of the workspace, we have the **Status Bar**. It's not something all that important; it shows some info about zoom level, selected artboard, and selected tool. Finally, in the center of it all, we have the **Artboard**. This is where you will add elements like geometric shapes, text, and images. The white rectangle is the size you selected when creating the document, and more than one artboard can be created, for a multi-paged file, like a presentation. If that's already overwhelming for you, don't worry, give it some time and you will get used to it.

Important tools and panels for starters

Now, we'll show you some of the most important tools and panels to get you started. One of the bases of graphic design is geometrical shapes, and that's where we'll start. Let's press the letter M to select the Rectangle Tool. All the Shape Tools work more or less in the same way, so we'll just explain the Rectangle. But remember, click and hold on the Rectangle Tool to bring the menu with the other shapes. To create shapes in the artboard you have two options: you can either click and drag and make the shape the size and proportion you want, or just click a single time, which will bring a menu where you can input the exact size you want. When clicking and dragging, you can hold the SHIFT key to lock the proportion to a perfect square. This also works with the other shapes as well, to create perfect circles or polygons.

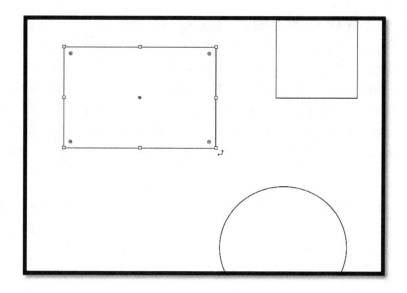

Now that we have something in the Artboard, we can talk about the tool you will use the most: the **Selection Tool**. There are two selection tools - the Selection Tool (keyboard shortcut V), and the Direct Selection Tool, (keyboard shortcut A), or the black cursor and the white cursor.

The Selection Tool (the black cursor), is used to select, move, rotate, and scale entire objects in the artboard. For moving objects, just click and drag them. For rotating, place the cursor close to the corners until it turns into this curved two-sided arrow. For scaling, use these white squares around the bounding box of the object. If you hold SHIFT while scaling, you will also keep the proportions.

Bonus tip: hold the ALT or OPTION key while dragging an object to duplicate it.

How shapes work in Illustrator

Now, for the Direct Selection Tool (the white cursor), we have to first take a look at how shapes work in Illustrator. Any shape in the Artboard is made up of points that we call **Anchors**. Two anchors connected make a **Path**. When the Path is curved, like in a circle, the Anchor Points will also have **Handles** to control the curvature. These three elements - Anchors, Paths, and Handles - can only be manipulated individually using the Direct Selection Tool.

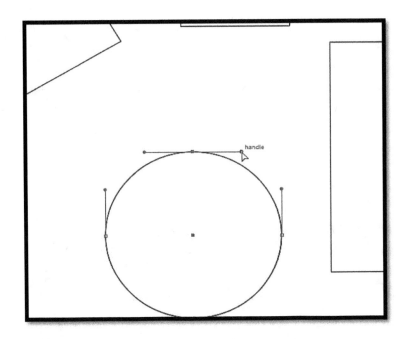

Let's draw a circle on the Artboard. Press the letter L to select the Ellipse Tool, then clicks and drags to draw a circle. Now, press the letter A to select the Direct Selection Tool, and hover the mouse on the top part of the circle, until the Anchor name pops up. Then, click and drag to move only that Anchor Point. Cool, right? You might have noticed that the Handles are also showing now. You can click and drag them to change the curvature of the Path. You can also click and drag on a Path to move it, but it can be a little tricky. What if you want to draw something more complex than just geometrical shapes? Well, then you'll use the Pen Tool. With the Pen Tool (keyboard shortcut P), each time you click on the Artboard you create an Anchor Point, which will be connected to the previous one, just as you can see in the **image below**.

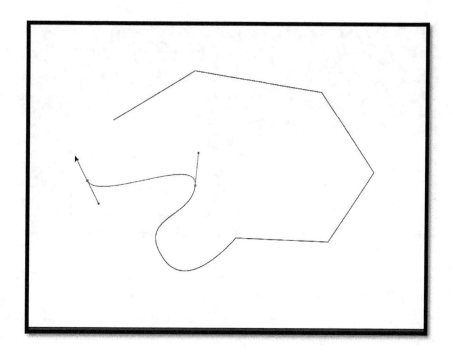

If you click and drag, you'll create a curved path. Clicking back on the first Anchor will close the Path and finish the shape. This tool can be a little bit challenging at first, it requires a little bit of practice to get used to, but it's a super important part of Illustrator and you'll use it a lot once you get the hang of it.

Moving around your workspace

Now, before we move on to Panels, it's important that you learn how to move around the Artboard. Which, lucky for you, is super easy to do? You can move around in lots of different ways, but our preferred methods are either to hold the Spacebar then click and drag, or to click and drag using the mouse wheel. For **zooming**, you can hold the ALT key, or OPTION if you're on Mac, then scrolls with the mouse wheel.

Getting familiar with the panels

Now, let's see a few Panels. The one you'll use the most is the **Color Panel**. It's already opened by default and of course, some panels do not display, by default, all their options. Click on the sandwich menu in the top right corner of the panel and click "Show Options". Now that's better.

The Color Panel is used to change the color of the shapes you create - both the fill color and the outline color, which you can switch by clicking on their respective icons right there in the Color panel. Then, all you have to do is select the object and change the color as you like. The next panel is one that you'll get to use all the time is the **Align Panel**. It's not open by default but you can open it in the Window menu. The Align Panel automatically opens the **Pathfinder** and the **Transform Panels** as well; they are more like a group. You can drag this panel to the right side and dock it on the Panel Bar. The Align Panel is pretty straightforward. Select the object you want to align and select the desired alignment, like center, left, or right. By default, when you select only one object, it will align to the Artboard. But if you have two objects selected, the panel will automatically switch to align to the selection.

Next in line is the **Pathfinder**. This panel is used to create new shapes by combining two or more shapes. You can unite two shapes into one, intersect the parts that are overlapping, or just divide everything into different shapes. It's really easy and really useful.

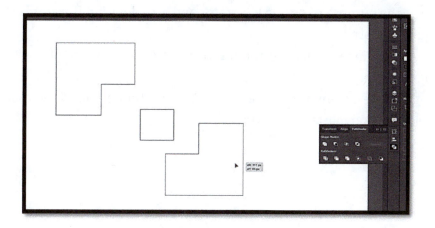

Finally, we have the **Properties Panel**. This right here can be your best friend if you get used to it. Just like the Control Bar, the Properties Panel is context-based, meaning its contents change depending on what you have selected. In fact, the Properties Panel is like an extension of the Control Bar, in a way. This is the only panel that you may have to expand at all times, and it is truly a lifesaver as it can speed your workflow in so many different ways.

27

Well, congratulations, you just learned the basics of Illustrator, but your journey is just starting.

Review Questions

1. What is the purpose of Adobe Illustrator and how does it differ from other graphic design software?
2. How can beginners navigate the interface of Adobe Illustrator to start creating their own designs?
3. What are the essential tools and functions in Adobe Illustrator that beginners should focus on mastering initially?

CHAPTER 3

GETTING FAMILIAR WITH THE WORK AREA

In this chapter, we're going to do a quick tour around the Illustrator Work area and show you some of the basics to get you started.

Opening a file

First, let's open up a file. With Illustrator open we'll go to File, go to "Open" and find the files that we've either downloaded or saved and would want to open. To open up a zip file you just need to double-click that and open it. If you don't know how to unzip double-click it and if you still can't do it just search unzipping on your computer and you'll get there.

Creating a new document

To create a new document head to the "New file" button on the left side and click it. Here you can input your artboard dimensions, the color profile, and quality. For this illustration, we'll create an HD artboard of 1920 x 1080 pixels.

Saving your documents

You can save your document by going to the File menu and clicking "Save as" or using the shortcut COMMAND/CTRL+S.

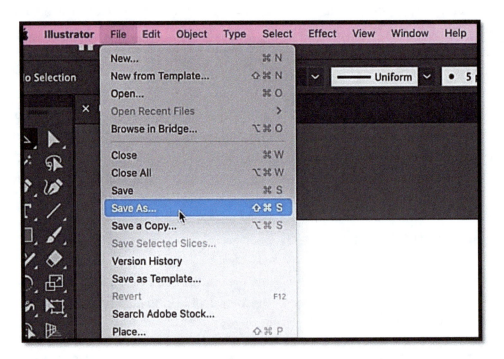

Configuring your workspace

After you open your file, your screen should look similar to what we have in the image below.

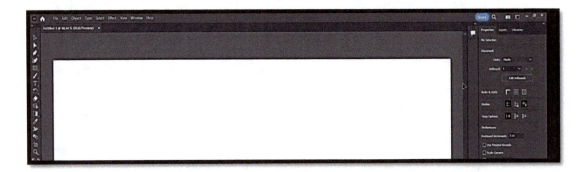

However, if it looks slightly different, there are a couple of things we want you to do just to make sure that we're on the same page when we're walking through it. At the top where it says Window, go down to "Workspace" and you should be on Essentials. Give that a click then go back here and reset Essentials just so that we're on the same page. The next thing is to set the Units. Some people prefer centimeters and millimeters while other people prefer inches. With nothing selected what we've got is a black arrow which is like the default thing that we normally go to as a tool. Click on the background in the gray area here. This means you have nothing selected and under the Properties tab, depending on where you are, click on the Properties Tab and where it says "Units" pick your unit of choice.

The next thing we're going to do for this course is to make our UI bigger. Currently, you'll notice that everything's quite small and you've got a lot of space but it's not good for these illustrations because you need to see everything and you might find this quite useful if you find everything's just too small to read. Go up to Illustrator, then to Preferences if you're on a Mac but if you're on a PC it's in a slightly different place and that is under Edit menu, at the bottom here you'll find Preferences so whichever one you're using, go to Preferences and find the option that says User Interface.

What we're going to do is indicate if we want it small, medium or large. We're going to choose Mega Large just so that you can see it easily as we proceed but be sure to pick the size you like. It'll say we need to restart Illustrator for this to work and we're going to say OK. Now if we go back to Illustrator we can see everything's bigger.

Navigating the workspace

After creating your document, this opens up the Illustrator workspace. On the left, you can find the Tools panel. On the right, we have panels like Layers, Colors, Gradients, and more which help manage your creations. You can hold the spacebar to pan around the artboard. You can also hit Z on your keyboard to activate the Zoom Tool and zoom in and out of your artboard.

The Layers panel

The Layers panel can be found on the right side of the interface. If you don't find the panel you are looking for head to the Window menu at the top and you can find the list of Property panels.

Layers allow you to keep your designs organized. You can create a new layer, rename them, and even rearrange them however you like.

Creating basic shapes

Let's now show you how to create basic shapes. From the panel on the left select the Shape Tool. You will find options to create rectangles, ellipses, polygons, and more. From this panel, select a rectangle tool and by clicking and dragging on the artboard you can create your shape. If you hold SHIFT on your keyboard then it will create a perfect square. The same goes when creating ellipses. To create a triangle, select the Polygon Tool, click anywhere on the artboard, input three sides and then presses ENTER.

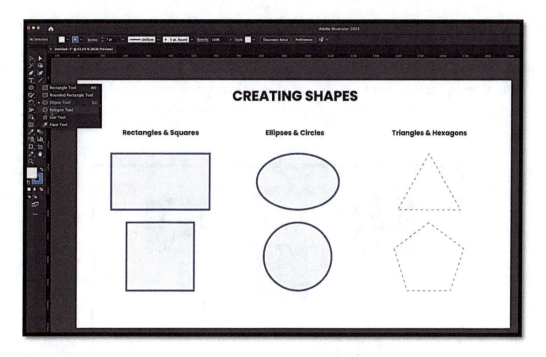

Selecting an object

To select an object press the letter V on your keyboard and this brings up the Selection Tool. You can then select your object and move it around your artboard. If you press the letter A on your keyboard you will activate the Direct Selection Tool. This tool allows you to select points to manipulate them and it also allows you to round off object corners.

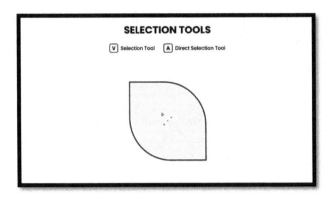

How to Select Multiple Objects

Here's a quick section on selecting multiple objects in your document. These could be a couple of objects such as shapes and a piece of text. There are different reasons why you want to select multiple objects, whether you're grouping them, you're aligning them or you're applying effects to multiple objects at the same time, but the quickest way you can do this is either by holding SHIFT while clicking different objects and this will begin to create a group selection.

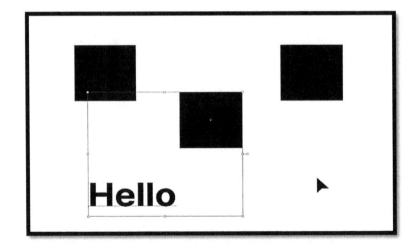

Let's say you clicked the wrong one on accident, continue to hold SHIFT and it will deselect whatever you click on if you already have that object selected so that's one of the quicker ways to quickly select very specific objects. If you want to select a bunch of objects in an area you can click and drag outside of your objects and it starts to form a Marquee and anything inside of that selection will be selected.

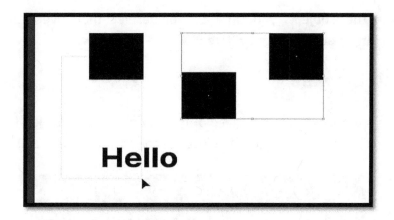

Now let's say we have two objects selected, we can click and drag to select another two while holding SHIFT and it will add that to the selection. The same thing applies in reverse, if we want to deselect two of those we simply click and drag and it's going to deselect those two. That's a way to select and deselect multiple objects at the same time rather than holding SHIFT while just clicking objects individually. You might notice in your Layers panel if you toggle down this layer group you just have a single layer with all objects on that layer; it shows which objects are selected by the little double circle over here so you can hold SHIFT and click on these layers as well to select different objects over here.

This is a different way of selecting, whether you hold SHIFT and select a bunch of objects in a row or you SHIFT click or COMMAND/CTRL-click to select individual objects. You can see that if you just click on each of these layers, it's simply selecting that object. If you hold COMMAND or CTRL on Windows it's going to select multiple objects and if you hold SHIFT it'll select a bunch of objects in a row. All of these objects are out here so if you had something named or you couldn't exactly click on it out here but you have layers in your

Layers panel with these objects, you can select and deselect them over here as well that's how to select multiple objects at once here in Adobe Illustrator.

Colors and Strokes

With the shapes created, you can assign color fill and color to the strokes by selecting the shape then head to the Color menu and select the color from your swatches to fill.

By pressing SHIFT+X on your keyboard you can switch between Fill and Stroke. You can give your shape a thicker stroke by going to the Stroke panel. Here, you can play around with the thickness, the caps, and the corners. The Pen Tool is used to create shapes and paths. Click to create anchor points and drag to create curves. You can also manipulate the curves later on with the Direct Selection Tool.

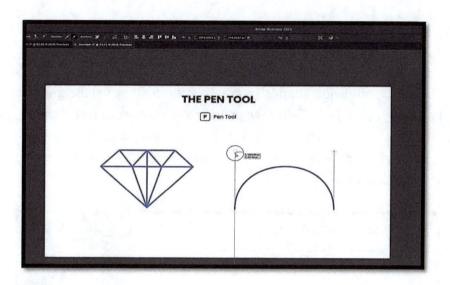

Adding Text

To add text, select the Type Tool from the Tools panel on the left, click on the canvas, and start typing. You can edit the font, the size, and more by using the Character panel. If you click and drag on the canvas you will create an area that will automatically be filled in with sample text. The type tool also offers options to type on any path and also within any shape area.

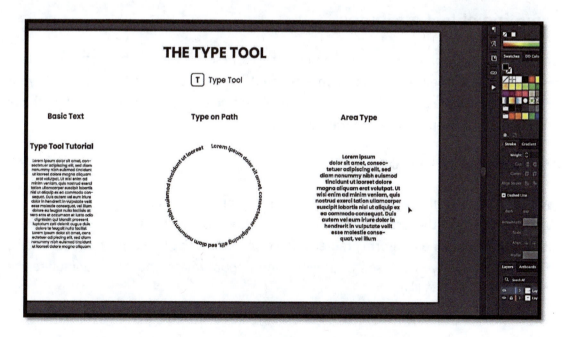

Manipulating Shapes

The Shape Builder Tool is a powerhouse feature in Adobe Illustrator. It allows you to combine, subtract, and divide shapes to create your custom vector graphics. Selecting multiple shapes together, press SHIFT+M on your keyboard to activate the Shape Builder Tool. With this tool selected, simply click and drag over gray areas to combine the shapes. To subtract shapes hold down ALT for Windows or OPTION for Mac and click or drag over the areas to delete them.

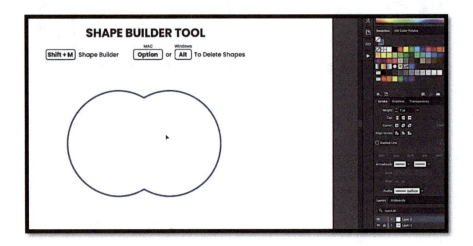

Sampling object attributes

The Eyedropper Tool allows you to sample strokes, colors, or any other attributes from one object to another quickly. You can activate the tool by pressing the letter I on your keyboard. To sample a color and stroke from one shape to the other, select a new shape and with the Eyedropper, click on the other shapes.

Apply color transitions

The Gradient Tool allows you to apply Color transitions to objects or shapes. Select any object and head to the Gradient panel; you have the option to add a linear gradient, a rounded gradient, or a freeform gradient. Once you select one you can press the letter G on your keyboard, you will see a gradient line popup where you can manipulate the gradient however you like.

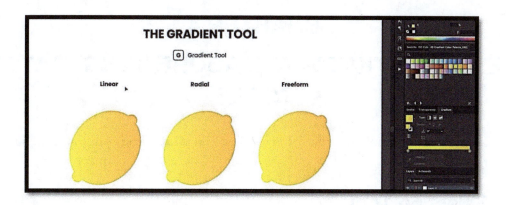

Isolation mode

The next thing we want to show you which is where a lot of people get lost really early is something called Isolation mode. We are going to fit an artboard to the window then we're going to group a couple of things together and then show you where you're probably going to get lost. We'll go to our Selection Tool, click this once, hold the SHIFT key down on our keyboard, click this once and we can select multiple things this way. So we're holding SHIFT down the whole time, just clicking a bunch of items and we can move. We've got them all selected, we are going to go to group so over here in our Properties panel there's an option to group or you can right-click it and there's an option to group. Now they are grouped, but if you love double-clicking you will get into the indicated area so if we click on this it's one unit but if we double-click it everything else goes washed out and it's no longer working. How do we go out? The easiest way to escape Isolation mode is to double-click the background and that gets us back out of it. So double-click to get in, double-click to get out. That's where you might get stuck. This has to do with things that are grouped and if you double-click things you'll end up in there so double-click to get in or with the little arrow here you can go back and it just takes you out as well.

Review Questions

1. How can you create a new document in Adobe Illustrator, including specifying dimensions and resolution?
2. How can the workspace be configured to suit your individual preferences?
3. What are the different panels available in Adobe Illustrator and how can they be used effectively during the design process?

CHAPTER 4

GETTING TO KNOW ALL ADOBE ILLUSTRATOR TOOLS

This chapter covers all the tools you'll find in Adobe Illustrator with a detailed explanation of what they do.

The Selection Tool

This is the most fundamental Illustrator tool and the one you'll spend the most time with. The shortcut is the letter V. It is used to make selections of entire objects, groups, and clipping masks, either by clicking or dragging. This tool is also used to move, scale, rotate, and round corners.

The Direct Selection Tool

The keyboard shortcut is the letter A. It is used to select and move individual paths, anchor points, and handles. It also selects individual objects inside groups or clipping masks, if they have a fill you can click on. Rounding corners is also possible.

The Group Selection Tool

There is no default shortcut for this tool. It is used to select objects inside a group without having to ungroup them.

The Magic Wand Tool

The keyboard shortcut is the letter Y. It is used to select objects with similar properties, such as color and stroke. It selects any object on your document, including the ones in groups and clipping masks. Options for the magic wand can be changed in the Magic Wand panel.

The Lasso Tool

The keyboard shortcut is the letter Q. It selects any anchor points inside the path drawn, including from objects in groups and clipping masks.

The Pen Tool

The keyboard shortcut is the letter P. It is used to draw paths. Each click adds a new anchor point to the path, and dragging the mouse before releasing the click will add handles for curvature. Clicking back on the first anchor will close the path.

The Add Anchor Point Tool

The keyboard shortcut is the plus symbol (+). It adds a new anchor point to a path.

The Delete Anchor Point Tool

The keyboard shortcut is the minus (-) symbol. It removes an anchor point from a path.

Bonus tip: if you hold the shift key while removing the anchor point, the path will be recalculated to stay the same.

The Anchor Point Tool

The keyboard shortcut is SHIFT+C. It is used to add, remove, or edit handles on an anchor point. Clicking on a curved anchor point removes the handles, and clicking and dragging adds them back. Dragging a handle with this tool will move it independently of the other one.

The Curvature Tool

The keyboard shortcut is SHIFT+TILDE. It is similar to the Pen Tool, but automatically creates curved paths.

The Type Tool

The keyboard shortcut is the letter T. With this tool, you can click anywhere to add text. Clicking and dragging will create a textbox. You can click on top of already existing text to edit it.

The Area Type Tool

This doesn't have any default shortcut. With this tool, you can click on a path to create text inside it.

The Type on a Path Tool

This doesn't have any default shortcut. With this tool, click on a path to create text that follows the path.

The Vertical Type Tool

There is no default shortcut. With this tool, click anywhere to create vertical text.

The Vertical Area Type Tool

There is no default shortcut. With this tool, click on a path to create vertical text inside it.

The Vertical Type on a Path Tool

There is no default shortcut. With this tool, click on a path to create a vertical text that follows the path.

The Touch Type Tool

The keyboard shortcut is SHIFT+T. This works similarly to the Selection Tool but with individual characters on a text. Click on a character to bring up the bounding box and then, you can scale, move, and rotate it.

The Line Segment Tool

The keyboard shortcut is the backslash. With this tool, click and drag to create a line.

The Arc Tool

There is no default shortcut. Using this tool, click and drag to create an arc.

The Spiral Tool

There is no default shortcut. With this tool, click and drag to create a spiral. Use the up and down arrow keys to change the number of cycles of the spiral.

The Rectangular Grid Tool

There is no default shortcut. Using this tool, click and drag to create a rectangular grid. Use the arrow keys to change the number of columns and lines.

The Polar Grid Tool

There is no default shortcut. Using this tool, click and drag to create a polar grid. Use the arrow keys to change the number of subdivisions.

The Rectangle Tool

The keyboard shortcut is the letter M. Click and drag to create a rectangle. Holding SHIFT will create a perfect square.

The Rounded Rectangle Tool

There is no default shortcut. Click and drag to create a rounded rectangle. Holding SHIFT will create a perfect square. Use the up or down arrow keys to change the roundness.

The Ellipse Tool

The keyboard shortcut is the letter L. Click and drag to create an ellipse. Holding SHIFT will create a perfect circle.

The Polygon Tool

There is no default shortcut. Click and drag to create a polygon with all sides the same size. Use the up or down arrow keys to change the number of sides.

The Star Tool

There is no default shortcut. Click and drag to create a star. Use the up or down arrow keys to change the number of points. Hold CMD or CTRL while dragging to change the size of the arms.

The Flare Tool

There is no default shortcut. Click and drag to create the light rays and the halo, and then click on the desired direction to add the light rings. The objects created already have blending modes selected, so you can just place the flare on top of an image or an illustration.

The Paintbrush Tool

The keyboard shortcut is the letter B. Click and drag to create a smooth path, which is more like a hand-drawn style. Holding ALT after you start dragging the mouse will create a closed path. Press the square bracket keys to change the brush size.

The Blob Brush Tool

The keyboard shortcut is SHIFT+B. Click and drag to create a filled, compound path. New paths will merge with existing ones of the same appearance if they touch each other. Press the square bracket keys to change the brush size.

The Shaper Tool

The shortcut is SHIFT+N. Click and drag to draw a rough approximation of the shape you desire, and Illustrator will automatically turn it into a crisp geometric shape. It works for straight lines, rectangles, ellipses, and polygons.

The Pencil Tool

The keyboard shortcut is the letter N. It works very similarly to the Paintbrush Tool. Click and drag to create smooth paths. Dragging the mouse close to where you started will close the path.

The Smooth Tool

There is no default shortcut. Click and drag over a selected path to make it smoother. It is also a nice way to reduce the number of anchor points.

The Path Eraser Tool

There is no default shortcut. Click and drag over a selected path to erase parts of it. This tool is terrible to use.

The Join Tool

There is no default shortcut. Select two open paths, then click and drag to join them.

The Eraser Tool

The keyboard shortcut is SHIFT+E. Click and drag on top of a selected object to erase parts of it. Press the square bracket keys to change the eraser size.

The Scissors Tool

The keyboard shortcut is the letter C. Click on a path to split it at that specific point.

The Knife Tool

There is no default shortcut. Click and drag over an object to cut it.

The Rotate Tool

The keyboard shortcut is the letter R. Click and drag to rotate the selected object. Clicking anywhere in the artboard will change the reference point of the rotation. Holding SHIFT will lock the rotation in increments of 45 degrees.

The Reflect Tool

The keyboard shortcut is the letter O. Click and drag to reflect the selected object. This tool can be quite confusing, the easiest way to use it is to hold shift and drag observing the reference point.

The Scale Tool

The keyboard shortcut is the letter S. Click and drag to scale the selected object. Holding SHIFT will lock the scale horizontally, vertically, or proportionally, depending on the direction you drag. Clicking anywhere in your artboard will change the reference point.

The Shear Tool

There is no default shortcut. Click and drag to skew the selected object. Clicking anywhere in the artboard will change the reference point and holding SHIFT will lock the tool on the horizontal or vertical axis.

The Reshape Tool

There is no default shortcut. Click and drag on a path to reshape it. This tool is clunky and can add lots of anchor points. There are better ways to reshape paths.

The Width Tool

The keyboard shortcut is SHIFT+W. Click and drag on a stroke to change its width at that specific point. The Width Tool adds handles, which you can move and edit whenever you want.

The Warp Tool

The keyboard shortcut is SHIFT+R. Click and drag to deform a path in the direction you drag.

The Twirl Tool

There is no default shortcut. Click and hold to twirl the object around the center of the brush.

The Pucker Tool

There is no default shortcut. Click and hold to deform the path towards the center of the brush.

The Bloat Tool

There is no default shortcut. Click and hold to deform the path towards the outside of the brush. It's the opposite of the Pucker Tool.

The Scallop Tool

There is no default shortcut. Click and hold to **scallop** the path towards the center of the brush.

The Crystalize Tool

There is no default shortcut. Click and hold to deform the object towards the outside of the brush, creating spikes. It's the opposite of the Scallop Tool.

The Wrinkle Tool

There is no default shortcut. Click and hold to wrinkle the path by deforming it randomly.

The Free Transform Tool

The keyboard shortcut is the letter E. Selecting this tool with an object selected brings up a menu with 3 different options - Free transform, Perspective distort, and free distort. With this tool, you can scale, rotate, shear, and add perspective to any object.

The Puppet Warp Tool

There is no default shortcut. Select this tool with an object selected to bring up a mesh used to distort the object. The mesh has control points that can be dragged and rotated. They can also be deleted by selecting them and pressing the Delete key, or added by clicking on the mesh. This tool does not add anchor points, so it is limited to distorting only using the already existing anchors.

The Shape Builder Tool

The keyboard shortcut is SHIFT+N. Click and drag through multiple paths to unite them in a single shape. Hold ALT and drag to delete paths. This tool works similarly to the Pathfinder.

The Live Paint Bucket Tool

The keyboard shortcut is the letter M. Select multiple objects and click using the Live Paint Bucket to create a live paint group. After that, you can click on any enclosed path to paint it with the selected color. You can also select a color palette on the swatches panel and switch between colors using the left and right arrow keys.

The Live Paint Selection Tool

The keyboard shortcut is SHIFT+L. It is used to select fills and strokes inside a live paint group. Each click will select either the fill, or the stroke, and not both, like a normal selection. Hold SHIFT then select more than one stroke or fill.

The Perspective Grid Tool

The keyboard shortcut is SHIFT+P. Selecting this tool brings up the Perspective Grid in the artboard. The grid angles can be adjusted with the multiple control points in the grid. While the grid is active in the artboard, objects will be created within a specific side of the perspective. The side can be changed in the icon that stays in the corner of the screen while the grid is active, or using the shortcuts - numbers 1, 2, 3, and 4. To close the grid, select the Perspective Grid Tool and click the X on the icon. You can also change the number of points of the perspective in the Perspective Grid menu.

The Perspective Selection Tool

The keyboard shortcut is SHIFT+V. This allows you to move objects inside the perspective. Moving objects with this tool will automatically scale and distort them to stay in perspective. While moving an object you can also use the shortcuts 1, 2, or 3 to change the perspective side.

The Mesh Tool

The keyboard shortcut is the letter U. Click on a selected object to create a color mesh. Each click adds a new point to the mesh, which can be painted a different color.

The Gradient Tool

The keyboard shortcut is the letter G. Click and drag on an object that is painted with a gradient to adjust the angle and position of the gradient, as well as the position of colors and transitions.

The Eyedropper Tool

The keyboard shortcut is the letter I. With an object selected, select the Eyedropper and click on another object to copy its colors. If you hold the SHIFT key, only the stroke or fill color will be applied, depending on where you click. The Eyedropper also copies transparencies and text properties.

The Measure Tool

There is no default shortcut. Click and drag to measure a distance in the artboard. The info panel will be opened. The panel shows the position of the start point, the width and height distances, and the distance in a straight line, and the angle of the measurement.

The Blend Tool

The keyboard shortcut is the letter W. Click on two or more objects to blend the shape and color between them. Objects are grouped after the blend is created, but can still be selected by using the Direct Selection Tool or the Group Selection Tool.

The Symbol Sprayer Tool

The keyboard shortcut is SHIFT+S. Select a symbol in the Symbols panel and sprays the artboard to create multiple instances of that symbol. To create a new symbol, simply drag the desired vector inside the Symbols panel. All the instances of the symbol will be grouped in what's called a Symbol Set.

The Symbol Shifter Tool

There is no default shortcut. With a Symbol set selected, click and drag to shift the symbols inside the group.

The Symbol Scruncher Tool

There is no default shortcut. With a Symbol Set selected, click and hold on a symbol to bring the other symbols close to it. To bring them far apart, hold the ALT key before clicking.

The Symbol Sizer Tool

There is no default shortcut. With a Symbol Set selected, click to scale up the symbols inside the brush area. The closer a symbol is to the center of the brush, the more it'll scale up. Holding ALT while clicking makes the symbols scale down.

The Symbol Spinner Tool

There is no default shortcut. With a Symbol Set selected, click and drag close to the center of a symbol to spin it.

The Symbol Stainer Tool

There is no default shortcut. With a Symbol Set and a color selected, click on the symbols to paint them with the selected color. Proximity to the center of the brush and how long you hold the click affects how much they'll be painted.

The Symbol Screener Tool

There is no default shortcut. With a Symbol Set selected, click on the symbols to make them transparent. Proximity to the center of the brush and how long you hold the click affects how transparent they'll be.

The Symbol Styler Tool

There is no default shortcut. With a Symbol Set and a graphic style selected, click on the symbols to apply the style to them. Proximity to the center of the brush and how long you hold the click affect how strongly the style will be applied.

The Graph Tools

All the graph tools work the same way, so we're going to explain them all together. The keyboard shortcut for the first graph tool, the **Column Graph Tool**, is the letter J. Click and drag anywhere in the artboard to create a graph with the desired size. A spreadsheet will appear where you can input the data that will be shown in the graph. You can also import data externally.

The Artboard Tool

The keyboard shortcut is SHIFT+O. This allows you to create, move, copy, and edit artboards in your document.

The Slice Tool

The keyboard shortcut is SHIFT+K. Click and drag on the artboard to create a rectangular slice. The artboard will be split into several chunks, which you can export separately using the "Save for Web" menu option.

The Slice Selection Tool

There is no default shortcut. This allows you to select, move, and resize slices.

The Hand Tool

The keyboard shortcut is the letter H. Click and drag to move across the artboard. You can also access the Hand Tool more quickly by either holding the Space key then clicking and dragging, or clicking and dragging using the mouse wheel. In both ways, you'll return to the previously used tool once you release the mouse click.

The Rotate View Tool

The keyboard shortcut is SHIFT+H. Click and drag to rotate the view in Illustrator. Holding SHIFT will lock the rotation in increments of 15 degrees.

The Print Tiling Tool

There is no default shortcut. Selecting this tool automatically turns on the visibility of printing tiles. By default, you will only have one tile in your artboard. To tile your document for printing, you have to open the Print menu and on the Scaling drop-down menu select "Tile full pages" or "Tile imageable areas".

This will tile your document in the selected media size. Hit "Done." Now you will have multiple tiles, which you can reposition using the Print Tiling Tool.

The Zoom Tool

The keyboard shortcut is the letter Z. Click to zoom in. Hold ALT and click to zoom out. Clicking and dragging sideways smoothly zooms in and out. These are all Adobe Illustrator tools. Many tools explained in this chapter have other features and functionalities besides the ones shown and you'll find out as you get better at Illustrator.

Also, virtually every tool will change its behavior when you hold SHIFT, ALT, or CTRL/CMD keys, so experiment with all of them. A lot of these tools will also open up customization menus when you hit the ENTER key with the tool selected, so experiment with that as well.

Review Questions

1. Explain 7 tools in Adobe Illustrator and give examples of how they are used.
2. How can you customize your toolbar in Adobe Illustrator to easily access your favorite tools?
3. Are there any lesser-known tools in Adobe Illustrator that can make the design process better? If so, how do you use them?

CHAPTER 5

CREATING A GREAT-LOOKING LOGO DESIGN

In this chapter, we are going to share with you the secrets behind creating a great-looking logo design. We'll be looking at the tools, techniques, and a few things to watch out for now.

Make a simple logo with shapes

The logo we'll be designing is a giant letter S with some gradients but if you are following along you can use any letter you like. With a new document open, we are going to select the Ellipse Tool then click and drag holding SHIFT to draw a circle. We'll drag holding ALT or OPTION to duplicate this and scale it up, select everything, and set the Fill to None. We'll move the top part a bit further up, select the Line Tool, and click holding SHIFT to draw a line.

Line up objects

First, we're going to look at lining up objects so we are going to select everything and align these centrally then holding SHIFT, we can move these up and down so the lines all connect.

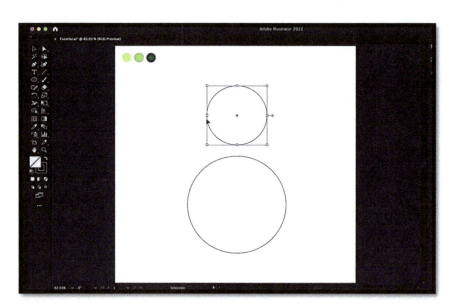

Now by holding SHIFT, we can use the main Selection Tool to extend this line and if we zoom in closely we can try and line the circle up with this line even more. If we press COMMAND or CTRL+Y we can jump into Outline mode and then select the Direct Selection Tool. We can then use this to move the Anchor Point out of the way and then pull it back and it will snap to this path. Make sure when moving this around that the line does not intersect with the circle.

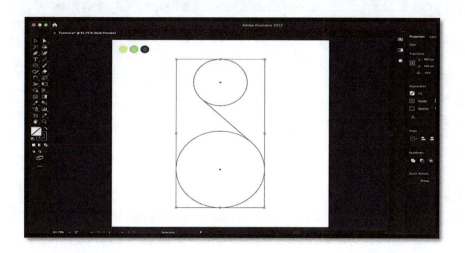

Let's do the same thing for the other end and the goal is to line these up precisely so we get a smooth letter S. Now we are going to thicken up that stroke a bit so it looks better.

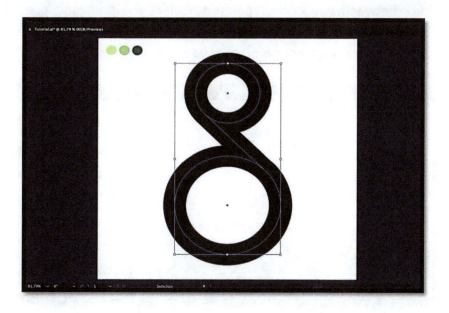

Make some cuts

Now it's time to make some Cuts along the path. We are going to select the Scissor Tool usually hidden under the Eraser Tool and we can click anywhere on a path to make a cut. By adding these cuts, we get more anchor points.

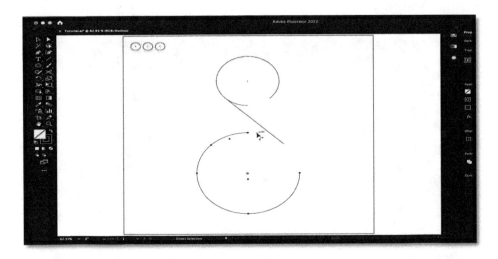

Remove anchor points

We're going to look at removing these anchor points so let's switch back into Outline mode and click between two anchor points to select the path and press Delete or backspace. If we do it again it removes a bit too much so we are going to undo that; make sure if you do find any stray anchor points that you delete those as well.

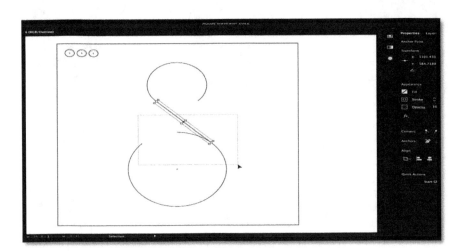

Now let's do the same for the bottom, which means we are going to drag over that segment and press delete or backspace. Make sure you get rid of any straight anchor points and then we can look at removing and merging segments so we nearly have a letter S.

Remove and merge segments

We are going to drag over everything and select the Shape Builder Tool, hold ALT or OPTION, and drag over a path to remove it. We need to zoom in closely on where the paths meet and to get around this we need to create a tiny bit of intersection. At this point, our smart guides keep snapping this to something annoying so we can turn those off with COMMAND or CTRL+U and now we can make this intersection slightly and if you have trouble selecting the path you want just press COMMAND or CTRL+2 to lock one path, select the other path and then unlock them after. Right now we know these paths are touching, we are going to select everything, grab the Shape Builder Tool, hold ALT or OPTION, and drag. Now if you've done this correctly you should have three separate pieces and we're going to join the paths together.

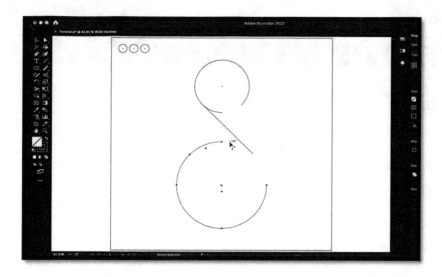

Join the paths together

Using the Direct Selection Tool, drag over those end anchor points, go to Object, down to "Path" and select "Join." Do the same for the other end so we have one long path and now we can round off the strokes.

Round off the stroke

From the Stroke drop-down we'll change the Cap type to round and this will round off those hard edges. If you'd like to trim them down a bit just grab the Scissor Tool, make a cut, and then delete the end anchor point just to trim it down a bit.

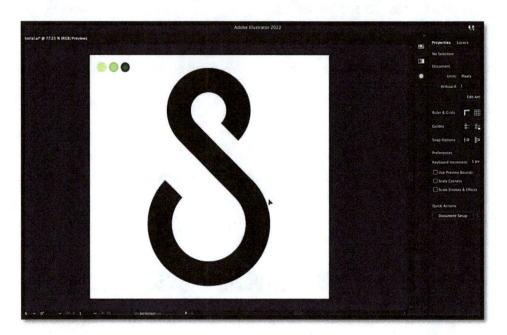

Extend paths

With everyone's favorite, the Pen Tool, we can select an existing anchor point, hold SHIFT, and click to extend the line. We're not using this technique this time but we wanted to demonstrate it because it is very useful. We are going to thicken up the stroke and just trim down the top section a little bit more.

Expand strokes

Let's look at expanding Strokes, so with everything selected go to Object, then to "Expand." leave fill and stroke checked and click OK and what this does is convert a stroke into a shape with a solid fill. Now using the Eyedropper Tool we can sample the light green and then move on to the next step.

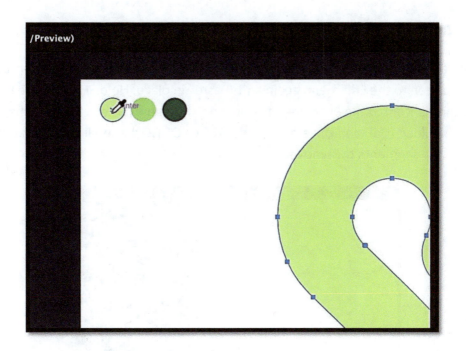

Use shapes to define new segments

Once again, let's select the Ellipse Tool and create a circle. We are going to make sure we have no fill and a stroke (making that stroke the darkest green) and we're going to adjust the size and position. We can then jump into Outline mode, zoom in nicely and closely, and line everything up precisely and the more you zoom in the better the result.

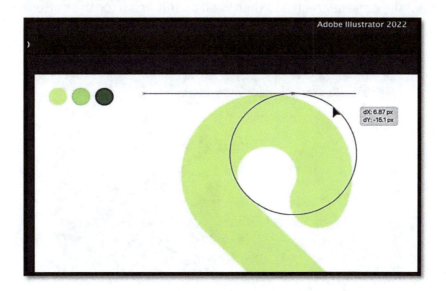

Separate shapes

Let's look at separating shapes. We are going to select everything, go to Edit down to "Copy" and then to the Edit menu again and "Paste" in place. Hold SHIFT on the keyboard and use the right arrow key to nudge the second shape out, select the first shape, grab the Shape Builder Tool, and once again hold ALT or OPTION and click and drag through part of the top segments to remove them.

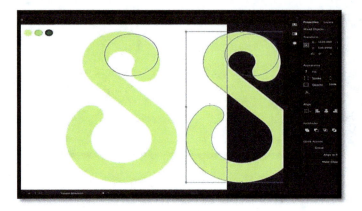

Now we need to do the exact opposite for the second shape so let's start by removing the pieces we don't need and then once you've done that you can let go of ALT or OPTION and just click and drag through the remaining segments. We can then hold down SHIFT and use the left Arrow key to nudge this back into position. We are going to give this added segment the darkest green and then we'll do this again for the bottom. For the bits of path leftover just make sure to remove them.

Apply custom gradients

Now let's apply some custom gradients for that we are going to select the main body and open up the Gradient panel, click on the slider to add the default gradient, double-click the black switch over to the Swatches tab, and then select the darkest green. Click anywhere on the slider to add another color. For this, we'll select the middle green, double-click the white, and then add the lightest Green. Now we can select those darker segments and then use the Eyedropper tool to sample that same gradient.

This does look a bit off so we are going to change the angle of this gradient, that way, we get the darker color on the left and just by doing this it makes a big difference. Now for that main body section, we are going to add a few more swatches and we'll have that lighter green right in the middle acting as a highlight. We are also going to adjust the angle and then delete these three swatches.

Add highlights

Now it's time to add some highlights. First, we are going to zoom out and then select the main body, hold SHIFT, and use the left Arrow key to nudge the new shapes out, add another copy to the right-hand side as well, and with the left one selected set the fill color to none and then make the stroke a bright right color (we'll go with magenta) and the goal here is to use the Direct Selection Tool to delete all of the anchor points except the ones that are where we want the highlight to appear.

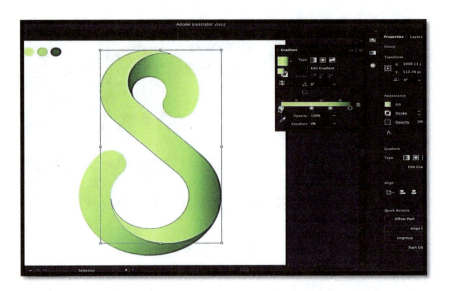

Once we've isolated those anchor points we can nudge them back into position and then zoom in nice and close. If you do have trouble selecting this path just nudge those other pieces out of the way and just to make life easier we can select that pink curve and make sure that this is at the front. Now let's thicken up that stroke and then from the Stroke panel we can change the width profile to something nice as this gives us a nice shape for the Highlight. We are now going to put it all back together and play around with some blending modes.

Blend altogether

Of course, we don't want this to be pink so we can select it and sample a different color like the gradient for example or we could just pick a color like white.

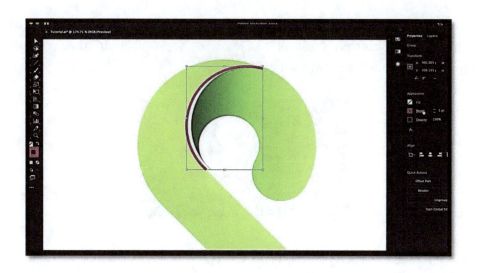

Now let's go and expand the appearance so the shape has a solid fill. If we hop into Outline mode we can see this shape has a line down the middle and if we start using blending modes to reduce the opacity we'll be able to see where the other shapes underneath meet and it will look a bit terrible so we are going to copy the top section and nudge it out, drag over everything to select, grab the Shape Builder Tool hold ALT or OPTION and click and drag over everything and then remove just one half of that curve.

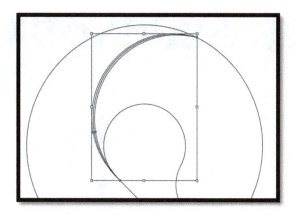

We can also trim off the ends if they're just a bit too fine and by removing half of this shape we've now made the Highlight thinner. If you'd like a thicker highlight, well just make sure you account for this earlier in the process when defining the stroke width. Now let's delete that solid white one and then nudge back in the new highlight and because this doesn't bridge where the two shapes underneath meet we can then change the blending mode to something like overlay or soft light and we can see this effect looks cool

63

as the colors of the logo underneath are also visible too. We are to do the same again and add a highlight to the bottom. After all is said and done, you should have something that looks like what we have in the **image below**.

Design Modern Logo Using Grid

In this section, we are going to show you how to design a logo with any individual letter. We will also show you the full process of making your logo modern. First of all, we are going to type the letter M which is what we are going to design. Make sure you are using Asgaard font then take the Line Segment Tool and draw a line. Give it a stroke color, now select the line and copy it by holding ALT and make a total of four lines by holding ALT and pressing D.

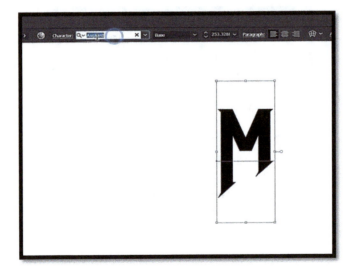

Now select the lines and group them. Now we need to copy the lines so go to the Edit menu and select Copy. Again, go to the Edit menu and select "Paste in place." Now rotate the line 90 degrees.

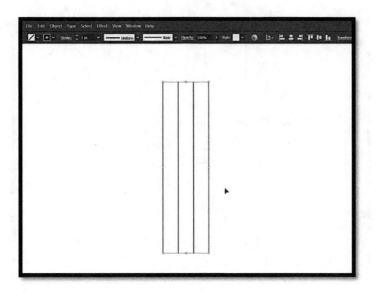

Next, select the lines, copy them, and move them a little bit aside. You can easily copy it by pressing CTRL+C and CTRL+F. After that, select the top line and make it smaller, changing the color as well.

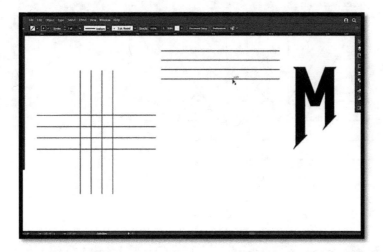

You can put the red lines on the other lines then select the red lines, go to Transform, and make it 123 degrees. Select both lines and make a group. After which you can select everything and make it align at the Center. Next, select the red lines and reflect the rotated ones. For reflecting, right-click on the mouse and select Transform then select "Reflect" and copy it.

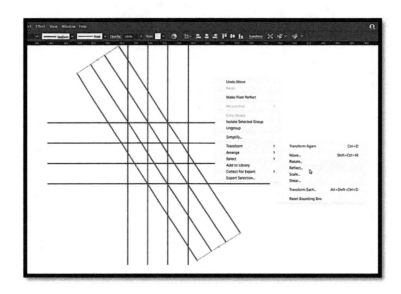

Now we are designing our end letter on these lines but before that, we have to check whether the top line is perfect or not so we'll go to Outline mode by pressing CTRL+Y.

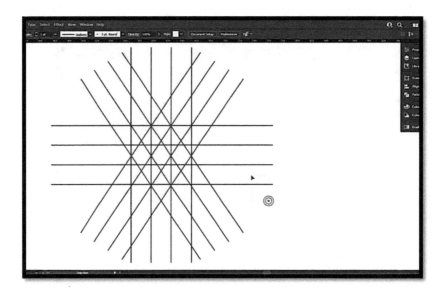

As we can see from the **image above** there is a little bit of a gap so we are going to match it. Now we can go back to normal mode by pressing CTRL+Y, selecting the lines, ungrouping them, and making the lines a little bit longer. At this point, we are going to select everything then take the Shape Builder Tool and also turn on the Fill color. We are going to draw the letter M (don't join the top part to the button part).

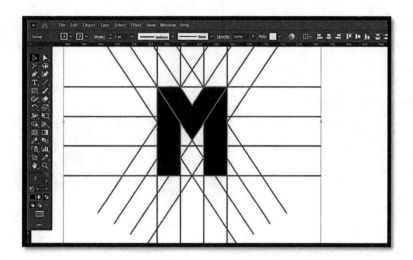

After we have successfully drawn the letter M we are going to move it above the lines but first, we have to ungroup it so we'll hold SHIFT, select the letter M, and move it above the lines. We can now turn off the stroke color of the letter M letter, then select the design and make it a group.

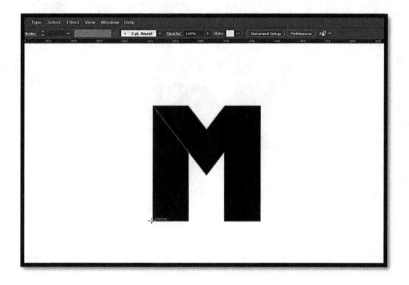

With the Rectangle Tool, we are going to draw a rectangle equal to the letter M and then we are going to change the color of the rectangle. We can also decrease the opacity. From there, we would select the rectangle, double-click on the curve point, and curve it how we want after which we would reflect the curve using the method we showed you earlier.

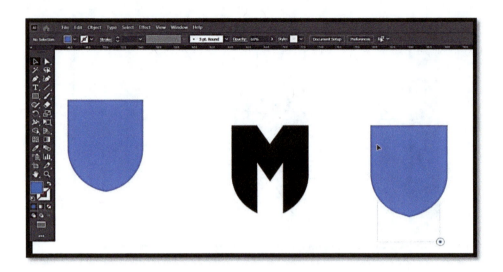

Select everything, take the Shape Builder Tool, and delete it. Next, move the rectangle above the design. Select the shield and change the color from fill to stroke color then change the color to black.

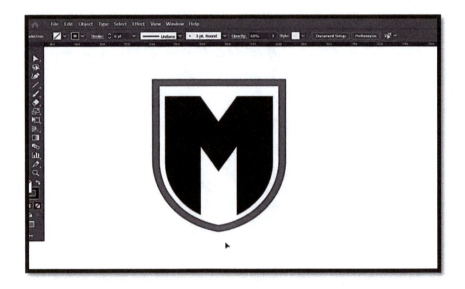

Select everything and make it Align Center. Select the shield and make it bigger. We can also increase the stroke color. Next, select the shield; go to Object and select "Path" then select "Outline Path." Select the design, take the Eyedropper Tool, and use the color of your choice. With the Rectangle Tool draw a rectangle equal to the artboard and send it back.

Now take the Pen Tool and draw the middle of the shape. We can also decrease the opacity of the part.

Select the part and reflect it by using the method we showed you then place it perfectly over the middle part. With that, we have completed our logo design.

Review Questions

1. What should you think about when creating a good-looking logo in Adobe Illustrator?
2. Give step-by-step instructions on how to use shapes, text, and effects to make a logo in Adobe Illustrator.
3. How can you make sure your logo looks professional and can be made bigger or smaller without losing quality?

CHAPTER 6

HOW TO MANAGE AND WORK WITH ARTBOARDS

Knowing how to manage and work with artboards is essential in learning the fundamentals of Illustrator. Working with artboards is an essential step in learning to use Illustrator more effectively. From resizing them to repositioning them, they can speed up your workflow so in this chapter, we're going to be taking a look at how to manage and work with artboards in Illustrator. A lot of times clients will ask for multiple versions of things and you want to make sure that they are happy so in this section, we are going to be looking at how to navigate, create, and edit artboards in Adobe Illustrator and then use these new skills to create design options for a holiday greeting card.

What is an Artboard?

An Artboard is the area that we are working on that when we export will show so think of this as windows. If we have a bunch of let's say different shapes that we are working on, the gray line we see on the interface is the artboard so if we click on that it is going to turn black and that means that it is now the active artboard, however, if we click on another one the previous Artboard goes gray and then the new one goes black.

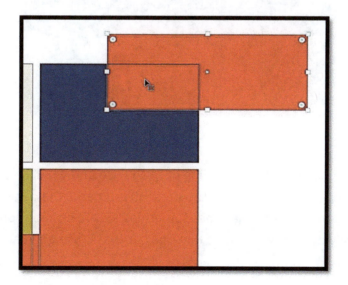

What you need to know is that the black outline of an artboard is the active one that you are working on and the reason you need to know what you're working on is if you select a shape, for instance, and then you want to align it to an artboard and start using your Alignment tools, it's aligning to the active artboard so you want to make sure that the artboard that you want is active and then you can align to that artboard. Another thing we want you to know about artboards is that you can make as many as you want within the document and artboards are also able to be resized and changed as you need.

Making changes to the Artboard

Now you've just created a 1080 x 1080 artboard for instance, let's say you want to make some changes to this artboard in terms of size, position, or shape. There are a couple of different ways that you can do it. The first way is using the Artboard Tool which is in the Toolbar or you can press SHIFT+O on the keyboard.

If you click on that you'll see the bounding box for the artboard appear and you can simply drag on the anchor points of the bounding box to resize and you'll also notice you got a little pop-up showing the size of the artboard so if you need it in a specific size you can get it using that but if you're trying to get something a little bit more precise there are a couple of different ways that you can do that and one way is using the Artboard properties in the Toolbar.

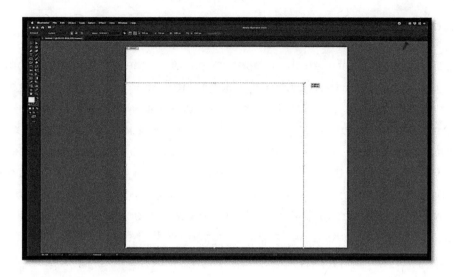

Changing the color of your artboard

We can change colors and adapt this to the way that we want it to look. If we want one that is all one color we can select the Artboard and just use the Eyedropper Tool to make it nice and bright. We can play around and do whatever you want with these artboards.

Artboard Properties

Depending on how you've got Illustrator set up you may find them in the Properties panel on the right here or in the control bar at the top if you have that turned on. If you don't have either of these options enabled you can find them under Window where you've got the Control at the top one and you've also got the Properties for the one on the right. With these, you can key in specific values for the width and the height of the artboard, including the specific size that you want so if you're looking for the 4 x 5 ratio for Instagram you can change that to 1350 and there you have the artboards ready for your 4 by 5 post for Instagram. You can also change the position of your artboard using the x and the y values on both these menus. You even have the option to choose from a specific template if you want a preset for the artboard size so if you're working on a specific design you can add that from the drop-down here. Let's say you want to do this for an iPhone X screen size, it will create a canvas at the right size for that application. If that isn't enough you can also double-click on the Artboard Tool like you can most tools in Illustrator to access the Artboard options.

Artboard options

You can also access this through the Properties panel on the right using the button here and once you've got the Artboard options opened up you have the option to rename the artboards. Again, you can choose from the presets if you want the size. You've got the width and height dimensions that you can key in, your position in the workspace and the orientation of the canvas so if you've got it set up as a portrait and you need it to be landscape you can switch that as well. You have the option to constrain the proportions of the artboard as you resize it, and you have the display marks where you can show marks, show the cross hairs on the canvas, and show a video-safe area. You also have an option for "fade region outside of Artboard" and we'll show you what that does in a moment.

If we hit on it, it just brings up all those guides that we've just enabled through the Artboard options so the fade region is for when you are resizing and you'll see the faded area around the artboard as that's showing you the size of the new artboard. This means the faded region just allows you to see it as you're resizing the artboard.

Working with multiple Artboards

Now you know how to work with one artboard, you need multiple artboards to work on a logo package, Instagram carousel, or something like that. If you need them the same size you can easily duplicate an existing artboard by selecting the Artboard tool and then if you hold ALT or OPTION and drag on the artboard you can quickly duplicate an existing artboard. So if you're working on a carousel and you want to position them right next to one another, you've got smart guides, you should be able to drag the artboard into place and let it snap when it touches or when it meets the other artboard.

Creating a new Artboard

You can also make a new artboard by using the "New Artboard" button in the Control bar up there or the one on the right here.

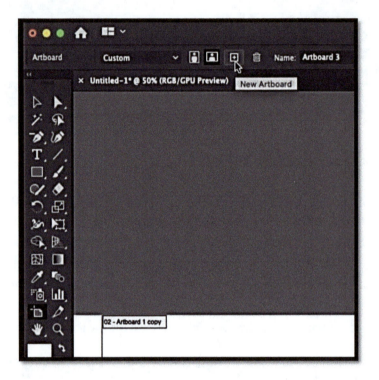

Resizing Artboards

Now you have multiple Artboards, let's say you want to resize them all to a different size - you can go through them manually and resize them all individually but you can also select each artboard, hold SHIFT as you're going through them, and select each one.

Rearranging Artboards

Any dimension changes you make to the width from the height up here, are going to resize the artboards there but you will notice they're all overlapping, and that is something that you can fix relatively easily. What you can do is to "Rearrange all" in the menu up here and from here you can choose the layout you want the artboards to follow, the columns that you want the artboards in, and the spacing between them.

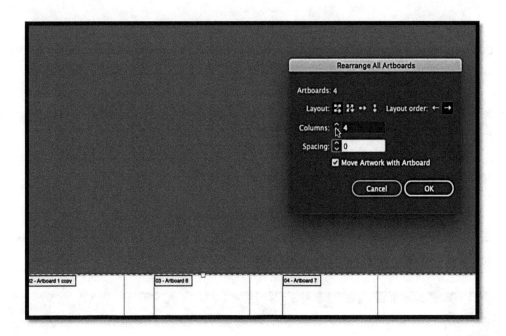

Let's say we want to create 0-pixel spacing between the artboards and we want them to go in a left-to-right fashion, in a column of four, we will set all that there and then hit OK. Now we can see that each of the artboards we created before has been positioned perfectly next to one another. This is handy if you're working on a project and it's got a little out of hand with the position of the artboards but it's also worth mentioning that it reorders based on the artboard number so if you created them out of sync they will remain out of sync but you can resolve this by heading to the Artboard menu which you can access in the Window menu. Select Artboards and what this will do is it will bring up a list of all of the artboards in your document.

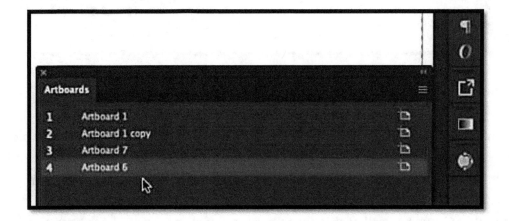

What you can do is rearrange the artboards to the order that you need them to be and how you want them to flow, only if you rename them so you know which artboard is which but if you already know which is which and the order that they need to go in, you can quickly and easily just drag them into the correct order, then just use the "Rearrange Artboards" option and that will then reorder the artboards to the correct artboard number.

Converting a shape to an Artboard

What if we want a shape to be an artboard? What if we are working in chaos and then we want one with a different size where we can throw some art on top of it? What we can do is click and goes to the Object menu, navigate to Artboards, and **convert to Artboards**.

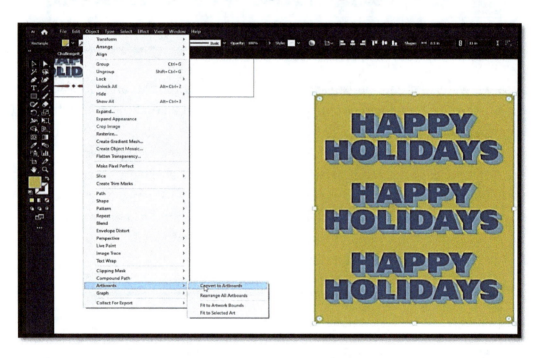

Now that shape that we had selected is an artboard so if you ever want to make your own shapes or your own sizes you can do that using the Rectangle Tool and you can click and it will bring up a dialog box so if we want an 8.5 x 11 which is a standard size piece of paper, we'll simply hit OK to confirm that. We can drop some art here like tile or something and if we want to export it we would click on the shape that we know is 8.5 x 11 because it says up here and we can go to Object, Artboards, and convert to artboard. The fun thing is we have all of this chaos but we can always come back here and click to reorder and this time we want it in three columns. We're going to hit OK and it's going to reorder all that artwork for us; it's going to move everything around and make it so that we can still work cohesively with all of these different artboards.

Exporting your Artboard

To export all of the Artboards that we've worked with at the same time we'll go to File, and then go to Export and then we're going to click on "Export for screens."

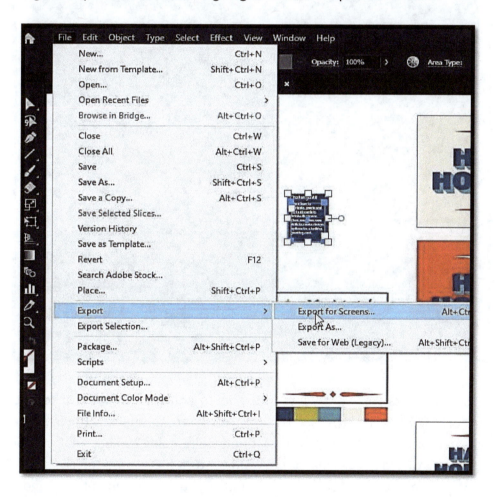

This is going to bring up a dialog box and when we're working with artboards we can usually do all of our naming here later. The options that we want are to include all we have and set it to go to the daily creative challenges folder.

You can select where you want yours to export to and then we want it to not create subfolders but we are going to export multiple versions of this right so this is where it gets exciting. We have 72 DPI for a PNG format and we're going to keep that one but then we're also going to add a scale, maybe we want to see a JPEG so we can click on JPEG 100 and now it has created JPEG 100. You can put in any suffix you can put here and you can put any kind of name that you want on there. You can also designate the scale so let's say the jpegs are going to be for print that means we want those to be at 300 DPI since the standard for print is 300. We can indicate if we want one more and we want these to be editable vectors so we can click on add scale then go to SVG and that is going to export it as a vector.

We can add a prefix here if we want and it's going to export as a challenge artboard so with the names what it's going to do is to export these names because it is exporting each of the artboards and keeping that name. The last thing we're going to do is hit "Export Artboards." If we go to view the files, we can see it has exported a jpeg, PNG, and an SVG of each of our different artboards including the names. We just exported a ton of different files without having to do much so as long as you name your artboards and keep them in check you can go over to File, Export, and Export for screens. Then you can fix up the names of your artboards and when you export everything will be named and sized in whatever you designate it to be right over here in this panel.

Review Questions

1. How do you make and change the size of artboards in Adobe Illustrator for different designs?
2. Why is it helpful to have multiple artboards, and how can you use them well in your design?
3. How can you move between artboards easily, and is there a way to share things between artboards in Adobe Illustrator?

CHAPTER 7

WORKING WITH LAYERS

In this chapter, we're going to talk about the Layers panel. The Layers panel is critical because you're going to use it a lot in everything that you do in Illustrator so you need to know how to rearrange layers, rename layers, modify specific layers, and do different techniques with them such as locking and hiding them so that you can see different aspects of your artwork. The Layers panel is important in helping you stay organized when you start creating designs especially when you have designs that have a lot of complex pieces to them or different aspects to them. You might have one image or graphic that you're creating but once you get into something more complex like a poster design and you've got titles, sub-headers, body text, graphic images, background images, and textures, it can get confusing and if it's all stuck on one layer it makes it even more difficult so we're going to show you guys just how to create layers, how to navigate through the Layers panel and how to move things around.

Accessing the Layers panel

On the right side of your workspace is a little double square stack which is the symbol for your Layers panel. Click on that to open that up.

If you don't have it in your workspace, go to your Windows drop-down menu. It's right there. Click on that and this takes you right away to your layers panel and now you can see you've got some options here.

Deleting a layer

Down below, the first symbol is the trashcan and that's obviously to delete a layer so if you're done with it or if it's blank or you don't need that anymore you can go ahead and just delete that.

Note: if you hit Delete and there's something in it like a leftover, an Anchor Point, or an image there that you're not aware of it'll give you a warning and say there's artwork in here, asking you to confirm if you want to delete this. This is a nice little feature just in case you forget something there.

Creating a new layer

The next little symbol, the square with the plus sign in it, that's how you create a new layer. Click on that and you can see a new layer pops up.

Creating a sub-layer

The next little symbol here creates a new sub-layer. So inside this layer, once you work on layer one and let's say you create a new sub-layer and then draw a couple of shapes here, you can see that layer has changed now. There's a little arrow symbol next to it.

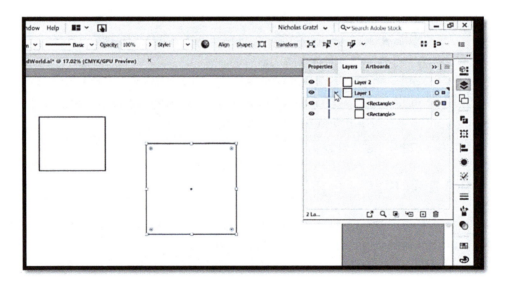

If you click on that arrow it opens up the sub-layers inside it so inside layer one there are two sub-layers which are those two rectangles you have drawn. Every time you create something on a layer it will add it as a sub-layer there, that includes guides, a single Anchor Point, type, or whatever it is, if it's on that layer that's selected it's going to put in there as a sub layer. This means if you're on layer one you can click on the little symbol right here and create a new sub-layer and it just puts one inside there.

Creating a Clipping mask

These next couple features you may not use as often but it is a way that you can create clipping masks. If you've got a shape here and you've got an image over the top, you can select the two and create a clipping mask of that shape or have that object in that shape. That's a nice feature but then we are going to show you another way you can use clipping masks.

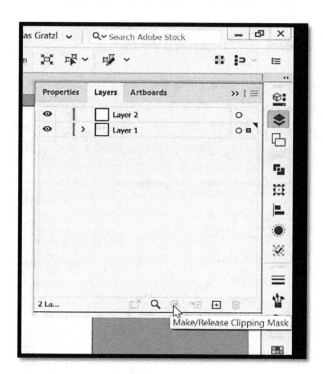

Exporting your layers

With the next two icons, you can collect all of your layers and export them as individual layers, and then you can also locate objects in your design using that feature.

Hiding your layers and sublayers

Coming up here to our Layers panel we want to point out a couple of things to you. First, you've got these little eyeballs - those are your visibility toggles. If you click on that you can hide whatever is in that layer and even more so when you open up this arrow in your sub layers you can hide individual sub layers if you want to.

This is a great feature if you're working on something and you want to see what is behind that, how to get that behind, how to move forward or what would it look like if it wasn't here so that's great for just experimenting with different things or you just need to hide it for a moment.

Locking and unlocking your layers

Next, you'll see there's a little blank square. If you click on that it adds a lock so now when you hover over this square they have that little pencil with the circle and a line through it says you can't do anything here because the layer is locked.

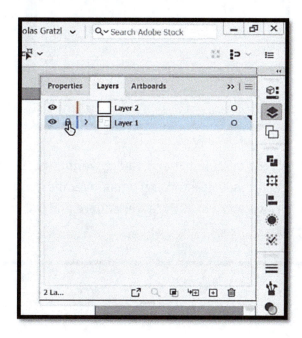

To unlock that just click on that lock icon and your square symbol comes up, you can now go to your Selection Tool, for instance, can click on any path and move that around or do what you want with it because it's unlocked.

Staying organized with Layers

Next, you'll see that little colored bar. This is cool as well - it's a nice little feature to help you find things so right now everything in that layer is going to have a little blue color to it and that's because it's in the layer with the blue box and what's even nicer than that - over here on the far right if you open up that layer you can see a little blue square pops up to let you know this is the sub-layer that you have selected right now so if you select a shape in another sublayer you can see that shifts.

If you've got a layer with a ton of stuff in it and you're wondering where a particular shape or element is you can find it easily. It'll tell you what layer it's in out here and then if you click on the sub-layer it'll give you a slightly larger square and tell you the exact sub-layer so it's nice for finding things.

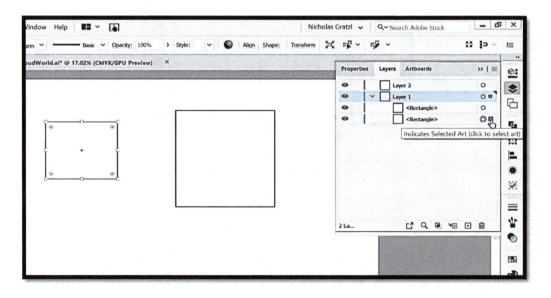

You want to try to stay organized when you get to more complex things since you've got a lot of things going on. Let's show you a quick illustration. We are going to go to Layer 2 and draw a circle or Ellipse here.

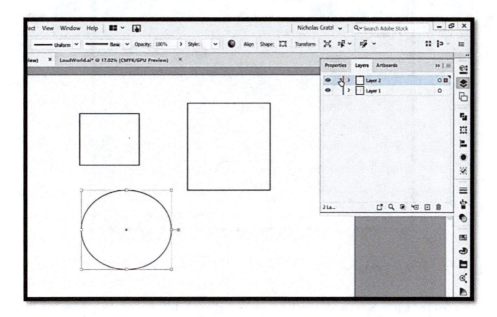

Now because this layer is red our bounding box and all our features for that circle are red. That's how it helps you keep track of those things so if we click on that red bounding box, we can see now it has an arrow because we have something in the layer which means there is a sub-layer that's the ellipse that we have selected.

Renaming your layers

If you double-click on the layer it opens up your Layer options panel and you can rename them. This is especially if you're doing some kind of an iteration process or you're doing a logo and you want to just iterate it more and more so you might want to label some things or if you're doing different variations you can rename each layer.

Changing the color of your layer

You can also change the color of that layer. Let's say your layer is currently light red but you want to change that to green, you can do that using this feature.

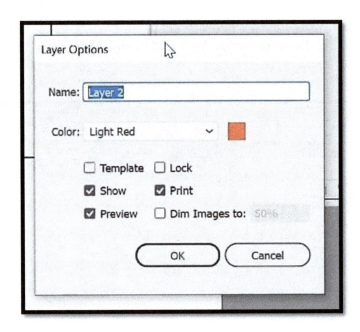

Creating a layer template

One other cool feature that we have here is the template option. You can use this when you bring a photograph into Illustrator so let's say you bring in a photograph of yourself and you want to do an illustrated self-portrait, you would create a new layer, place that image on that new layer, and then come in here click template and then what that does is it dims the image 50% and it automatically locks that layer. A simple explanation for this is taking a photograph, putting a piece of tracing paper over it, and having it locked down. Right now you can't do anything on that layer which means you can't draw on top but if you create a new layer on top then you can begin tracing and doing the work you have. That's a nice little feature if you want to trace a photograph of something else since you can just create a template and it locks it and puts it all in place for you.

Review Questions

1. Why do we use layers in Adobe Illustrator, and how do they help organize complicated artwork?
2. How can you create and organize layers in Adobe Illustrator to work efficiently?
3. Are there any special layer features in Adobe Illustrator that can help with editing or selecting specific parts of a design?

CHAPTER 8
WORKING WITH COLORS

Do you want to learn how to create beautiful color palettes or how to find the right shades for your shadows and highlights when you're drawing Vector illustrations? In this chapter, we are going to teach you how to easily create color palettes and show you how to draw and color your illustrations on Adobe Illustrator. There are two color modes: one is RGB and the other one is CMYK. What if you find out that your document is CMYK and you want to switch it to RGB because the client is asking for RGB or you accidentally used the CMYK mode and now you want to switch it to RGB? We will show you exactly how to do that.

How to create custom palettes

We have here on our canvas a few color swatches. What we have is the lightest color we want to use in our illustration and the darkest but we need to find the colors that would go in between the mid-tones.

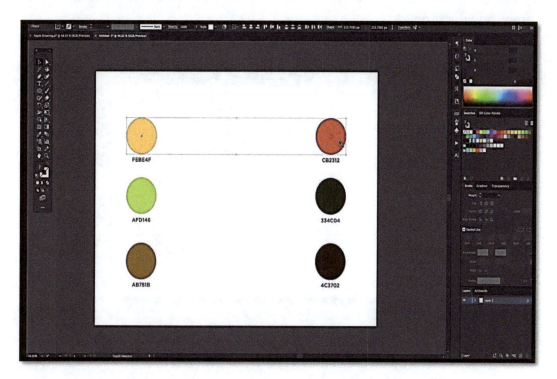

For that, we'll head over to the Object menu at the top and select "Blend." Under "Blend" we'll go to the blending options, click on the drop-down menu, and make sure we have "**Specified Steps**" selected. We'll change the unit to 3 so we have three mid-tones. Then we'll confirm by clicking on OK, selecting the yellow color and SHIFT click to select the red color as well. We'll go back to the Blend Tool and select "Make."

This will automatically create the mid-tones between both colors. We'll do the same for the green and the brown.

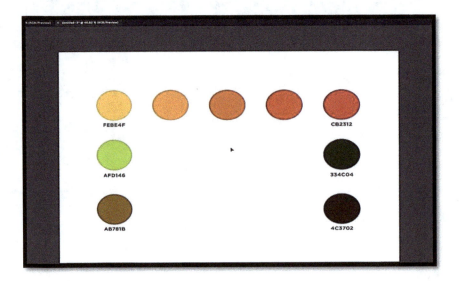

Now to turn these circles into actual shapes we'll head back to the Object menu, select "Expand." With object and fill selected, we'll click on OK.

How to use the color palette

Now that we have the Color palette created let's show you how to use them to color in illustrations. For the outline process, we will use our simple Shapes and Pen Tool style to outline the illustration and after that we're ready to add the colors to the illustration. Firstly, we'll select all and head over to the Layers panel holding OPTION or ALT on your keyboard. We'll drag the colored layer down to the other layer to create a duplicate, lock and hide the outline layer. On the Color layer, we'll delete all small unnecessary lines and details from the outline then select all and outline the stroke.

Head over to the Pathfinder panel and press the "Unite button" to merge all of your little shapes. Now release the compound path and delete the outer top shape here.

We are now ready to turn on the outline layer, select each individual shape, and apply a mid-tone color to it. Using the darker colors we can assign the Shadows which will go towards the bottom right of the illustration. We'll ensure you add some dark deep shadows and for the highlights we'll apply a lighter tone towards the top left of the illustration. There you have it. This is how to use your color palettes to create some beautiful vibrant Vector illustrations in Adobe Illustrator.

How to change color modes

In this section, let's take a look at how to switch between RGB and CMYK color modes. Firstly, when you start any new document in Illustrator by clicking the "New file" button or going to "File," and then selecting "New," in the dialog box at the bottom there's a Color mode selection. With this, you can select between RGB and CMYK.

Let's say we had CMYK selected when we created our document or you've opened a new document that you need to reselect the color mode. If we go up to File or Edit, depending on if you're on Mac or Windows, there's a document Color mode setting right here. It puts it right there for you and you can switch between CMYK and RGB just like that. You may have some CMYK photography or imagery in your document or something embedded so it might give you a warning but that's how you can switch those color modes.

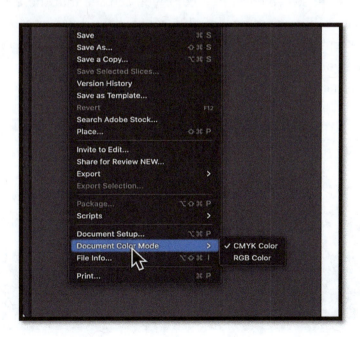

One other thing to show you here if we go up to Window, down to Color, our color out here could be displayed in a few different ways. This shows CMYK values but if we click the little hamburger menu we can switch what is shown and how we select our colors or pick our colors so we could switch it to RGB if that's what we want and now we have the HEX code down here and RGB values to work with.

So if your color guides here shows CMYK but you're in RGB color mode you can flip that right there. That's just an extra little bit and that's how to change color modes here in Adobe Illustrator. After switching to RGB color you can see that there's a change in the gradient and that is because some of the colors have been recalculated. You can immediately see that the white light is sharper here in the RGB mode. If you want to check which color mode you are in you can go to the document tab and in the parenthesis, it will show you which color mode it is in.

How to add a color swatch group

Do you want to know a quick way to speed up your design process? When saving color palettes in Adobe Illustrator, instead of adding each color separately as a new Swatch which will slow down your process you can select all of your desired colors, press "Add a new color group" then press OK, and now you can access all of your colors in one place.

Review Questions

1. What are the different ways you can change the colors in Adobe Illustrator?
2. How do you make and save your own color choices in Adobe Illustrator so you can use them again?
3. Give examples of how picking the right colors can make your design look better.

CHAPTER 9

WORKING WITH TEXT

In this chapter, we're going to be learning how to add and manipulate text in Adobe Illustrator. For this illustration, we've downloaded a vector image and opened it in Illustrator. Before adding text to this image we're first going to open the Character and Paragraph panels from the Window menu - this will allow us to easily control the font size, style, and alignment.

Entering your text

Click the Type Tool within the toolbar and then decide what kind of text you wish to add. For a single line simply click somewhere on the document and begin typing. For Paragraph style click and drag a text box within the document and start typing. You can then use the Selection Tool to resize your text box by dragging its corners.

Repositioning your text

You can also reposition your text by dragging the object anywhere on your document. Once you've entered your text, use the Character and Paragraph panels to modify your font size, line spacing kerning, and alignment. You can select text and use the color picker to change its color.

Adding text from your computer

A quick way to add text that's already on your computer in a text file such as a TXT or Microsoft Word file is to go to "File," "Place," then choose the text document from your computer and click "Place."

Make any necessary changes in the Options window and then click OK. Now click and drag a Paragraph text box within the document and your text will automatically be placed inside the box. Note that if there isn't enough room to show all of your text within the box a small red plus box will appear toward the bottom right corner indicating there is additional content not being displayed.

Modifying your text

Now let's move on to modifying text. Let's say we want to change the layout of our text and have it follow a path or a curve. We'll start by drawing a simple path using the Pen Tool then we'll reselect the Type Tool and hover near the left edge of the path. You'll see the cursor change to indicate text on a path. Click and then you'll be able to type directly on your path.

The cool thing is you can use the Direct Object Selection Tool to modify any points on your path and the text will automatically follow. Let's say we're unhappy with a character within a font or we simply want to modify the appearance or reshape some characters, we can have Illustrator convert the text into editable objects. First, we'll enter the line of text and then go to "Type," and "Create outlines" and Illustrator will then convert each letter into its own shape. You can then use the Direct Selection Tool to modify any of the points on any character.

Keep in mind that after you create outlines Illustrator will automatically group all your characters to keep their spacing in alignment. If you wish to move individual characters more easily simply select the text then go to the Object menu and choose "Ungroup." It's important to note that after you convert your text to outlines your text is no longer editable and here's a quick pro tip for you: converting text to outlines is also the best way to ensure your text will always appear properly when exported to any vector format. This is because Illustrator will not have to attempt to embed font files, some of which cannot be embedded and would require the user to have the font installed on their machine within your document. Instead, your text will simply be made of regular vector shapes and objects. There's a lot you can do with text inside Illustrator and these are just some quick and easy tips to get you started.

How to Use the Retype Feature

In this section, we're going to take a look at the Retype function in Adobe Illustrator 2024. For this illustration we have a file where we have prepared some images, these are pixel images that we have created, and a photo of the packaging but then this type is a little distorted. We all know that it's Lobster, but let's see if Illustrator knows that as well. And then we have our own fonts used in these files, but they are installed on the machine. We have an Adobe font that is uninstalled. We also have Bickham Pro and have some OpenType features as well. Let's see what it does.

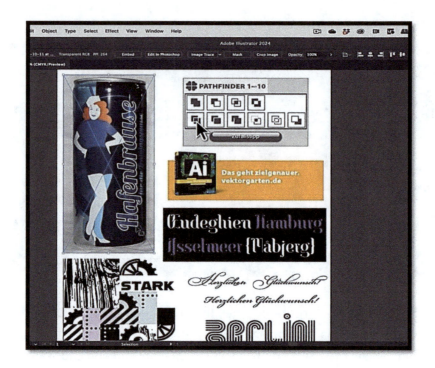

Now to enter it we are going to select the artwork, which is either a pixel image or an outline font. Then go to Type > Retype (beta).

You can also open this window from the Window menu and down there is Retype (beta), but let's go in here and open it. We can see it recognizes some text here and even on the photo that is inside that image and it sees all that text and creates several dotted lines around them. That's because they are all different fonts or they are recognized as different individual words.

Now we can click on them and see the fonts that Illustrator recognizes in there and if we think they are not matching, then we can find some more. This comes up with options that are ordered in the order in which they match best. In our case, we used Myriad Pro, because we just didn't go far to create these and Illustrator found some similar ones that look quite like Myriad. In case you want to have something special, then you can just use that. We will click on the one we want to have. We can double-click that text here as the pop-up shows which then notifies us that Illustrator wants to download some additional parts to this. Once the download has finished, the Retype feature is ready to use. Now we can double-click that and after applying the font it has now converted this to live text, so we can now exit this and then we can edit that. Also, we should be able to select another one of these and again find the matching font. Let's go with another Myriad one and apply that. Again, it has been converted to live text, so let's go in here and do that as well. After that, we'll see which one matches here. We're going to take anyone and apply as well and now we can see what Illustrator makes of it. Just to check this out, we see Illustrator has even edited that photo and hidden that previous pixel text. We'll move on to check out the other ones. With the panel open, we'll go in and enter that but then it's saying text recognition failed and that's because it's distorted. This means Illustrator recognizes some fonts and doesn't recognize others for various reasons. But now you know how this works you can go ahead to use it and have fun with it.

How to transform text prompt into Vector Graphics

Introducing the all-new "Text to Vector Graphic" feature in Adobe Illustrator. In a new, empty document, you won't initially find "Text to Vector Graphic" in the contextual taskbar. Instead, you can access it from the "Properties" panel or the "Text to Vector Graphic" panel. After using this feature once, it will become available in the contextual taskbar.

To access "Text to Vector Graphic", simply look for it in the Contextual bar, the Properties panel, or under the Window menu. By default, the output style will match the style of the active artboard. To change the setting toggle off the "Match active artboard style". Also, you can use the "Style Picker" to choose a style from an existing vector or image. Later, you can fine-tune your output level of detail from "Settings".

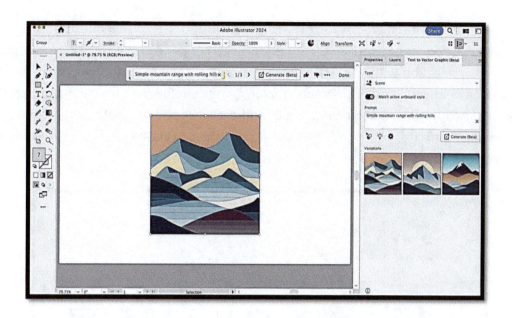

Now, let's generate a scene. Describe your vision and hit the "Generate" button. First-time users, make sure to agree to the user guidelines. Stay connected to the internet to avoid errors. Once connected, click "Generate" and you'll receive three variations. The first one is added to your artboard.

In the Contextual taskbar, use arrows to preview and select the one that suits your artwork best. Your generated vector graphic is neatly organized in groups for easy editing. Refine your selection with the Gradient tool or adjust the colors to your liking. Need to add a subject to your artwork? Draw a rectangle placeholder, then type in a description of the desired output in the prompt field and click "Generate." You can customize the color shapes, and size, as desired. You can also create icons effortlessly using this feature. It's versatile and adapts to your design needs.

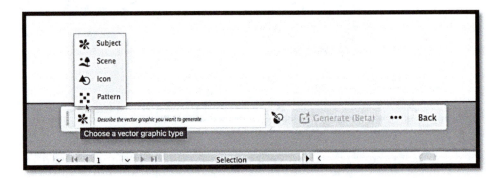

Finally, let's explore "Text to Pattern". Type in a description of the desired output in the prompt field and click "Generate." Ensure your instructions are accurate; any spelling mistakes can lead to errors. We've already created a path using the Pen Tool, meticulously outlining the sofa seating cushion. Now, let's add a pattern from the generated variations.

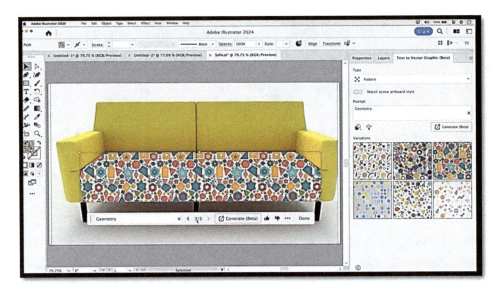

To enhance the outcome further, let's play with blend modes. Go to the Transparency panel. Here, add a blend mode; for instance, we chose "Multiply" and this beautifully blends all the textures and shadows, just like it would in real life. These options allow you to incorporate details from the raster image, such as lighting effects, curves, and distortions. Explore the "Presets" and "Color controls" to refine and limit your output colors.

You can even incorporate your brand's color palette using this. With endless possibilities and use cases, we can't wait to see what you create.

Review Questions

1. How do you add text to your design in Adobe Illustrator?
2. Explain how to make the text look shadowy or have a cool-colored background in Adobe Illustrator.
3. How can you change the text appearance without losing the ability to change their size or look?

CHAPTER 10

HOW TO EDIT ILLUSTRATOR TEMPLATE

In this chapter, we are going to show you how to edit Illustrator templates like replace images, color change, and make a file ready for printing.

How to replace images

If you want to replace images then you need to open the Link panel. Go to Window then click on the "Link" option.

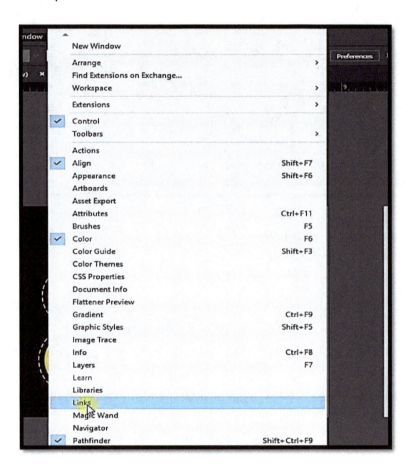

First, select the Direct Selection Tool, click on the image then go to the Link option and click on "Relink."

Now select the image and click on "Place."

How to change color

If you want to change color then select all objects using CTRL+A. When all objects are selected go to Recolor Artwork and change the color.

How to make a file ready for printing

When your file is okay and you want to make it ready for printing then you need to save the file as pdf format. To do that, go to File click on "Save as" and select Adobe PDF.

Now select high-quality print, click on "Marks and Bleeds" as checking the trim marks and bleed is most important for printing, then click on Save.

How to open a template

Open your Adobe Illustrator; you can see the Menu and Tools panel. Now go to the File menu, click on Open, and select your template. This will open your file in the illustrator.

How to edit text

If you want to replace or edit a particular text then go ahead and open the Character panel. Go to the window and click on "**Character**." Now select the Type Tool, make a selection of the text, and type or paste it here. You can control the text size and style from the Character panel.

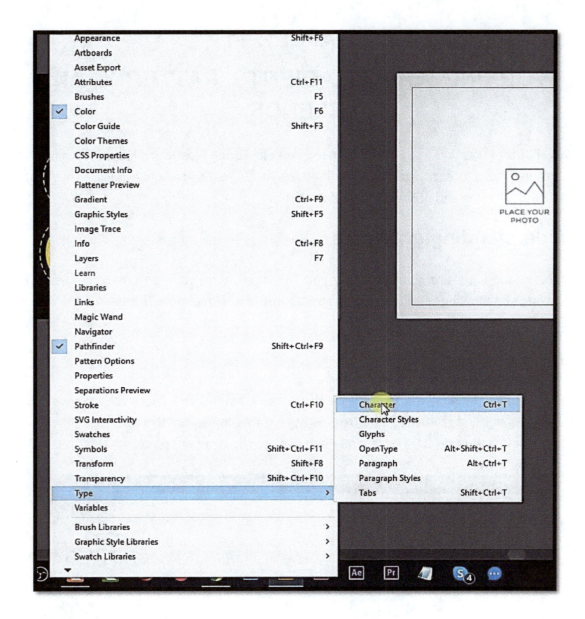

Review Questions

1. How do you change an already-made Illustrator design to fit what you want, like changing the colors or moving things around?
2. Are there any important tips to keep in mind when changing Illustrator designs to make sure everything looks good together?
3. How can you make an Illustrator design template look like it's yours?

CHAPTER 11

WORKING WITH GRADIENTS, PATTERNS AND BLENDS

This chapter takes you into more advanced work in Adobe Illustrator. Here, we will cover topics like how to easily use the gradient tool and create gradients like a pro, create beautiful patterns and utilize the blend tool.

Understanding gradients

In this section, we are going to show you the three ways you can create gradients in Illustrator by showing you these three famous app icons (Facebook, Tinder and Instagram) as examples.

Linear gradient

Let's begin by showing you how to use the linear gradient. The Facebook logo we have here has a vertical gradient going from light to dark blue so for this illustration, we will copy it, select the gray area here, and head over to the Gradient panel.

We will click on the first option which is the linear gradient and this will assign the logo a default white-to-black gradient transition.

Let's now apply the custom colors to it by going into the Color palette. We will select a light blue and just drag it on top of the white dot on the Gradient panel. We will do the same for the dark blue and this will apply the correct colors to the logo.

Now the example here has the color transition going horizontally so let's change that. We are going to press the letter G on our keyboard to activate the Gradient Tool then just click at the top, hold SHIFT on our keyboard, and drag down the gradient, and simply enough, we have created a linear gradient.

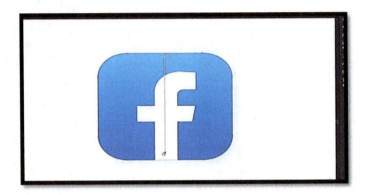

Radial gradient

The radial gradient is just as easy as the linear one. This gradient has its color transition starting from the center outwards. For example, we have the Tinder logo which we are using for this illustration. We can see the subtle transition from orange to pink.

Let's select the example here, head over to the Gradient panel, and click on the Radial option. From the panel, we are going to apply the orange color to the left side and the pink color to the right side. Then we'll select the Tinder logo and activate the Gradient Tool by pressing G on our keyboard.

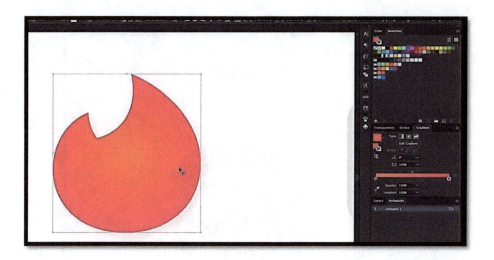

Once again, we'll click towards the bottom left and drag out the gradient upwards and there we have it.

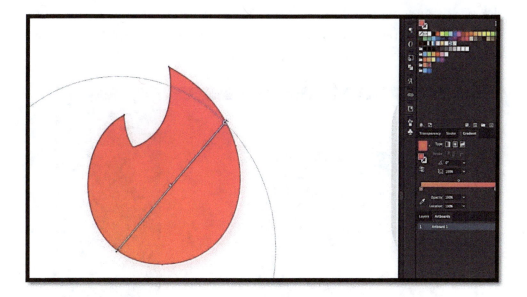

Freeform gradient

Lastly for this section, we're going to show you how Instagram created this beautifully colored logo with the freeform gradient. As you can see there are more than two color transitions and they all start from different areas but then, let's show you how to do this.

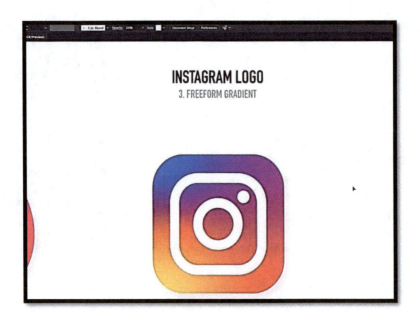

First, click on the gray logo head over to the Gradient panel, and select the third option which is the freeform gradient. As you can see here the circle will appear over the shape. We can assign a color to it or even add multiple circles.

Let's begin by placing the circle at the top left and assign a blue color to it then, just assign colors from the color palette where you see fit to copy the Instagram logo. To add more circles all you have to do is click elsewhere and there you have it.

Using the Gradient tool

If you have the Gradient Tool selected you can also add a type of gradient. We have three types: linear gradient, radial gradient, and freeform gradient. Linear gradient is easy - it's going to go from one to the other and with the Gradient Tool you can select where that starts and stops. Now with this Gradient Tool selected if you look at the line drawn across here in the middle we have a beginning color and an end color. The gradient itself goes between the furthest colors so if we bring white in, the gradient only starts where this color exists after that it's all pure white same with the black, you can tell after this black it's all just that swatch so if we bring this out, our gradient is going to run from one end to the other.

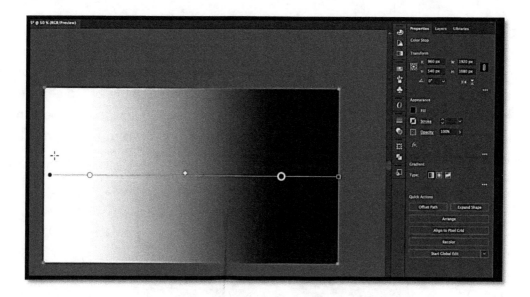

The little black dots allow you to adjust where the edges or the bounds of that gradient are. The one on the left moves it and the one on the right allows you to scale in and out, and you can always redraw that gradient if you want to. The diamond in the middle is basically which color has more influence on this gradient so it starts to transition a little slower until it hits this diamond and then it translates a little quicker to black or vice versa. The other thing you can do is Click the three dots under the Properties panel and you can see your gradient right here. You can add colors to it. Simply double-click on that gray and change it to a color of your choice. You can also change the colors here by going over to these color swatches and double-clicking on them which opens up your Swatches panel or the Palette or a Color Picker.

Adding transparency to your gradient

If you want to color-pick the gray color out here you can do that by selecting the color of your choice. You can even adjust the opacity as well so what if you want to go from red to the same red but you want the red on the left to be more transparent you can just double-click on that and change the opacity to zero and press return or click outside of that box.

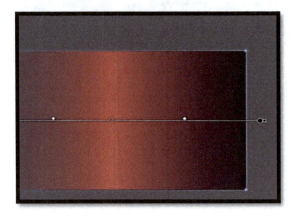

Now it looks like white but if you click and drag the shape up you'll notice that it's not white and that you're seeing white because your background color is white, meaning it's transparent. So no matter what color is underneath it you can see it a little bit better with the gray and you can see it when it overlaps here, how it goes from red to transparent.

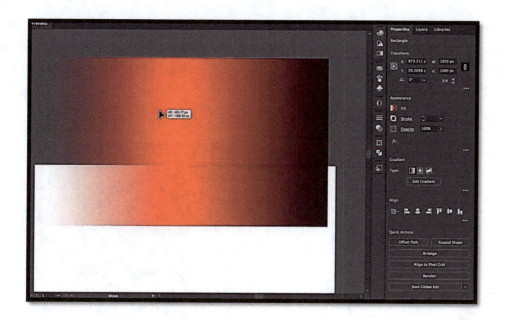

Manipulating your Gradient

If you want to get back to edit this gradient make sure the Fill is selected. You can grab the Gradient Tool and everything pops up again or you can see the Gradient feature over here in the Properties panel and adjust the gradient here with these three dots. You can change the angle of your gradient and that adjusts depending on where you draw it. You can remove a Swatch just by clicking and dragging it a little bit further down. You can also click on it and click the trash can to remove the Swatch as well.

This gradient can be applied to a stroke or fill if you want it. You can also have the gradient Swatch but if you increase that stroke weight to something a lot larger like 50 you can see how that gradient applies to the stroke. Now because you switched those swatches you could apply it to both if you wanted to just by clicking and dragging so there's a gradient on the fill and a gradient on the stroke.

You might have to make some adjustments here if you want it to be the same as each other or you would just include the gradient on one or the other, in this case, we're going to look at gradients on the fills so we're pressing G for our Gradient Tool again and now that you know all the basics we can switch this gradient to a radial gradient. Radial gradients are going to start from the center out in a circular pattern.

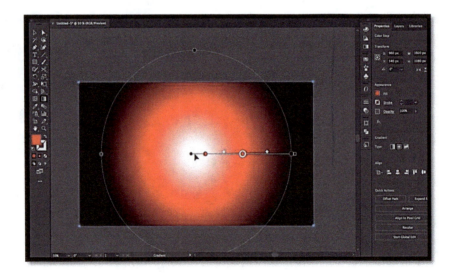

The last gradient we have to talk about is a new one called the freeform gradient. We also call it a Mesh gradient. What it does is it adds points out here that are like their own little radial gradients with a blur.

You can adjust the intensity of each of these points so you can have multiple gradient spots and you can see you have a little plus icon which means you can click and add another point. You can also change the color of those points by double-clicking on them and grabbing a different color from your swatches. You can move these points around to wherever you want these gradients to apply, you can click and drag their intensity which is how much these influence the other points. Bring them closer to each other and they'll all just blend. It's a cool way to create gradients here with this Freeform Gradient Tool.

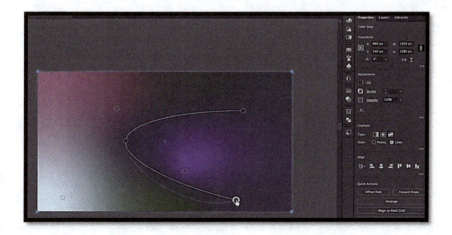

Our gradient tool defaults to just adding points but you can add lines and what that means is from one point or one gradient Swatch to another you could add a line and that's going to create some definite interesting effects here within your Freeform gradient. Press the ESC key to stop that line and then you can change how these gradient points affect what's going on and how the different points blend here in your gradient. It's a really interesting way to add different effects here to the gradient. Another thing here is that you can change the opacity of the different points as well to show a little bit of the background.

How to make a gradient blend

In this section, we are going to show you two ways of making multi-color gradient blends that you might not have thought of before.

Method 1

First, we're going to do a gradient blend, and this will take two different gradients and blend them. On one side, we're going to have an orange and a pink gradient, and on the other side, we'll have a purple-to-yellow gradient. To do that, we're just going to get on our Gradient Tool and also bring up our Gradient panel over here. Now, if you're not seeing the Gradient panel, you can come up under Window, and it'll be under there.

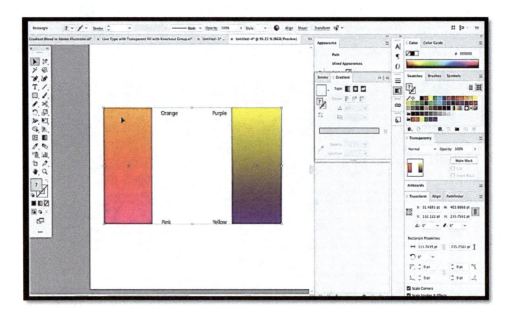

Next, we're going to click right here on the Gradient to give us a white and black gradient then we'll double-click here to set our color. Going into our palette, we are just going to choose, we'll go with orange, then click our other color which is pink. We'll change it to 90 degrees. So now we have our orange-to-pink gradient. We are getting back on our Selection Tool because we don't want a stroke, so we'll bring that to the front and then just get rid of it. Now, since the first one is already set up, we're going to delete it and just make a copy of the second one, holding SHIFT and OPTION or ALT and dragging. We'll get back on our Gradient Tool, and then just change the colors to purple and yellow. You can also do that right here in the Properties panel. Now we'll select both of these and blend them. To do that, we're going to come here to the Object menu and go to Blend and Blend Options.

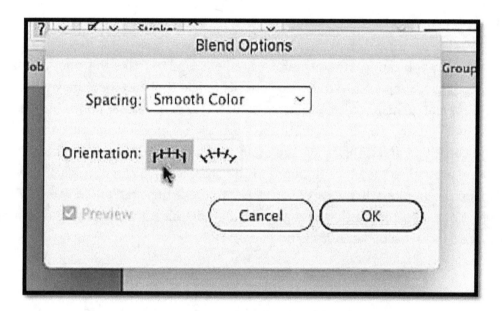

We just want this to be Smooth color, and it doesn't matter the orientation on this since it's two squares, and then we'll say OK. Sometimes your smooth gradients work, at other times they seem inconsistent. So if we want a smooth-looking gradient, all we have to do is go to the Object menu, select "Blend and Blend Options," change this to "Specified steps," and we can make this about a hundred, and we'll say OK. Then we'll go over to Object > Blend and Make. You can also hit SHIFT + COMMAND + B or SHIFT + CTRL + B on a PC. And now we have the beautiful gradient that we are expecting. So that's the first way of making the multi-color gradient.

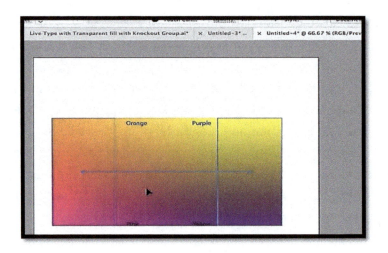

Method 2

The second way you can try is the freeform gradient, and to make this one, you can just make a rectangle. Simply hit M to get to your Rectangle tool and then draw a box. Next, in your Gradient panel, you're going to choose the very last option which is called freeform gradient and now it automatically starts with a gradient, giving us four nodes. Now, the cool thing about this is we can double-click these to change our color; we can move them around so they take up more of the area, and we can even click down here and expand the gradient that way. We are going to make this gradient look pretty similar to the first one. We'll make that orange, and then double-click the first one to make it yellow. We'll include a darker purple, and pink.

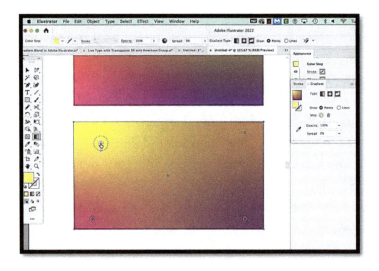

124

Now we have two very similar multi-color gradients, but they're just made differently. One cool thing to do with these is to overlay white text as this gives it a nice effect. Also, because these are made differently when we expand them, we get two different results. Let's go to Object > Expand Appearance to show you what we mean, and then we'll do Object > Expand. We'll expand the object and fill, and we have the option to change this to a gradient mesh but we'll just go ahead and tell it to do 255 objects, and we'll say OK.

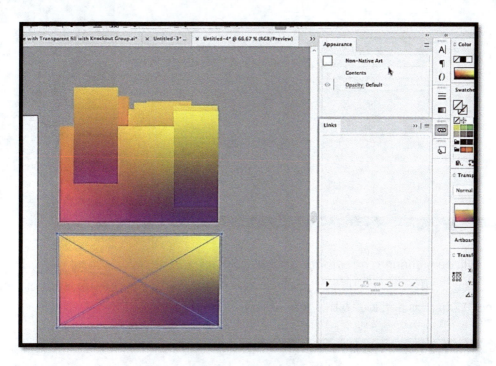

Normally when you expand a gradient, you get a lot of little pieces. You can hit COMMAND+Y or CTRL+Y to toggle in and out of Outline mode so you can see the difference here. If we use our Group Selection Tool, all of these are different pieces. And now, this one has been changed to something called non-native art; it changes it to an image, and just like all gradients, this may cause printing problems, so just be aware of that.

Create Editable Gradient Text

In this section, you will learn how to create editable gradient text in Illustrator. Type in some random text, then scale this up and change the font if you want. Now if you apply a gradient to this text nothing will happen, even though Illustrator might be showing that there is a gradient. What you have to do is just cancel out the gradient and you'll see that the text is there but it's invisible. Now go to the Appearance panel and add a new fill.

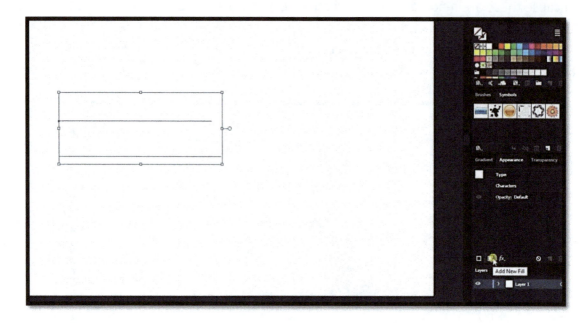

What it will do is change the color of the text to black and now you can go to gradient and just click on it. After that, you can apply some colors; if you change the text you will see that the gradient is applied to this text as well.

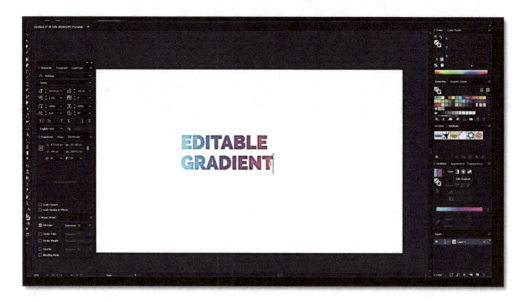

Working with patterns

Have you ever wondered how patterns work in Illustrator and how you can create one? If your answer is yes then you're in the right place. In this section, you will learn all that you need to know about patterns in Adobe Illustrator.

Accessing your in-built Patterns

Before you start to design your own patterns you should know that Illustrator comes with a nice set of patterns that can be easily accessed from the Swatches panel. If the Swatches panel is not opened you can easily do it by going to Window in the menu bar and selecting Swatches. To get access to your built-in patterns all you have to do is click the Swatches button, go to Patterns and here you will find the lists of patterns that come with Illustrator.

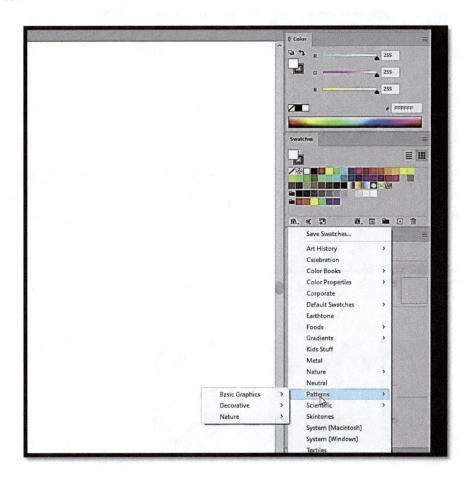

Select one and Illustrator will open a new panel where you can visualize and select the desired pattern. Keep in mind that by using these arrow buttons you can easily navigate to the next or the previous pattern collection.

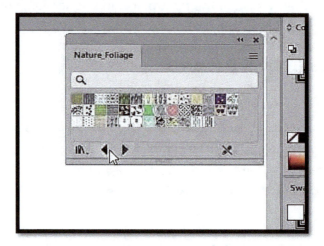

To use one of these patterns, you need to first select it which will add it to your Fill. If you select one of these vectors shape tools it creates a new shape that will be filled with your selected pattern.

Adding patterns to shapes

To add a pattern to an existing shape you need to select that shape and then click the pattern that you wish to apply for the fill or even for the stroke. You can see every new pattern that you apply gets added inside the Swatches panel which makes it easier to use it again.

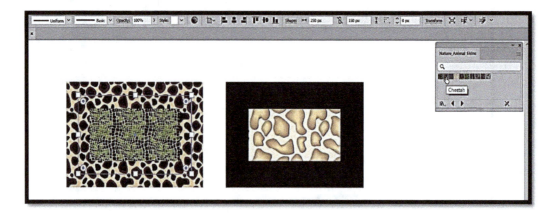

Applying a pattern to a text

Applying a pattern to a piece of text can be just as easy. Select the Type Tool from your toolbar and type in your new text or select a piece of text that you already have. Make sure that you have the "Fill" selected then click the pattern that you wish to apply.

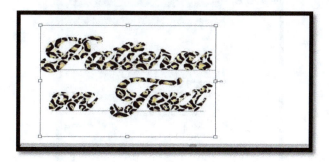

Creating your custom pattern

These built-in patterns can be really useful but in some cases, you might have to create your own pattern. Illustrator comes with a dedicated Pattern-building tool in the form of the Pattern options panel. You can easily open this panel by heading over to Window and "Pattern options" and by default your panel should be inactive. To use all the functions from this panel you have to select the artwork that you wish to turn into a pattern.

Open the pattern menu and go to "Make pattern." This will save your pattern inside the Swatches panel and bring up editing mode. In this mode, you have access to all the settings from the Pattern options panel and a live preview of your pattern. The original tile keeps the full opacity while the copies are a bit dimmed.

Editing your pattern

Now that your pattern is saved let's have a closer look at this Pattern panel and see how you can edit your pattern.

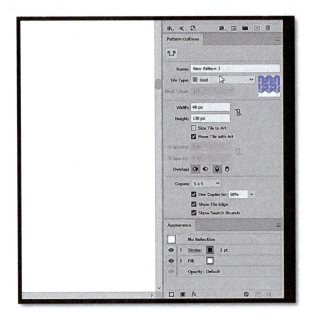

In the name box, you can type in a name for your pattern. From the File Type drop-down menu, you will decide the tile type and how the tiles should repeat. When you choose Grid, Brick by Row or Brick by Column, your tiles are treated as being rectangular while when you choose Hex by Column or Hex by Row, your tiles are fitted as being hexagonal.

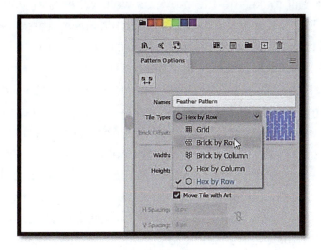

Selecting the Brick by Row File Type will give you access to the Brick Offset function. This setting lets you offset your tiles and you can choose between eight different values which produce different results. If you wish to scale your tile you can do it by adjusting the values from the Width and Height boxes or by clicking the square button which will activate a bounding box around your tile and now you can manually adjust your tile.

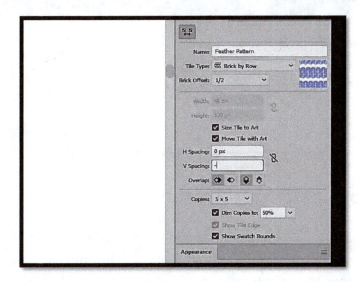

Whenever you increase the size of the tile beyond that of the artwork, Illustrator adds space which will increase the spacing between tiles. When you decrease the values, the tiles end up overlapping. To remove any unwanted overlapping returns to the original size values. All you have to do is check the "Size tile to art" box. The other box ensures that moving the artwork will make the tile move as well. Whenever you have the first box checked you can adjust the spacing between your tiles using these two values. Entering negative values will make your tiles overlap which takes us to these next settings that let you decide which tiles should appear in front when your tiles overlap. Moving to the bottom of this panel, the "Copies" settings can be used to set the look of your pattern preview. From this menu you can select the number of copies that should make up your pattern preview, you can increase or decrease the opacity of these copies or completely disable the dim effect. Finally, with the two boxes below that, you can turn on and off the visibility for the tile edge or the Swatch bounce. The Swatch bounce displays the portion of the artwork that needs to be repeated to create the actual pattern design. It might help you to better understand how patterns work as it allows you to see exactly where your shapes need to be for the tile transition to appear seamless. When you're done editing your pattern make sure that you click the "Done" button to leave editing mode and then you can use one of the Vector Shape tools to create a new shape that's filled with your pattern.

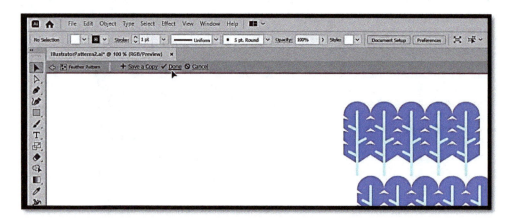

Creating your pattern from scratch

Now that you're familiar with the basic pattern-building techniques let's see how you can create your own wave pattern from scratch. Start by selecting the Ellipse Tool from your toolbar. Click on your artboard to create a 66-pixel circle, remove the stroke color, and select Fill. Change the color to 71, 87 and 94 and then go to Object, "Path and offset path." Set the Offset to -4 pixels. Click OK to create the new shape, change the color to 88, 239, and 255, and go again to Object, Path and Offset path, but keep the offset at -4 pixels. Click ok to create the new shape.

Grab the Eyedropper Tool from your toolbar and use it to fill this new shape with a color. Continue to use the same technique until you get to the center of the circle. Go again to Object > Path and Offset path, and keep the offset at -4 pixels. Click OK and fill the new shape with this color.

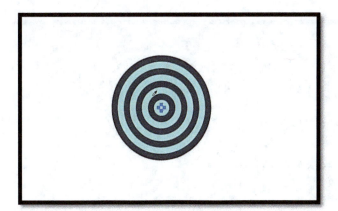

Now switch to the Move Tool so you can select all these circles that will serve as your pattern tile. Go to Object > Pattern > Make, to save these shapes as a new pattern and open the Pattern options panel where you can set the settings of your pattern.

You can name it Wave pattern. Select Brick by Row for the tile type, lower the width to 62, the height to 30 pixels, and keep the rest of the settings as they are. If you wish, you can play with the "Overlap" settings to adjust the direction of your pattern. Once you are done, click the "Done" button to save the settings for this new pattern. Select one of these Vector Shape Tools then create a new shape and fill it with your new pattern.

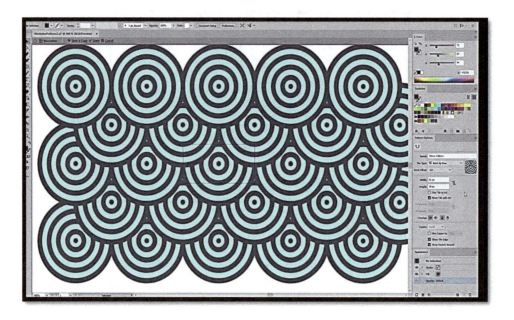

Scaling your patterns

Once applied, you might want to scale your pattern and if you try the classic method you might notice that the pattern does not scale. This happens because of a setting from the general menu that you can easily enable or disable by going to Edit > Preferences > General. Check the "Transform pattern tiles" option then click OK and now if you try to scale your shape you can see that your pattern scales with the shape.

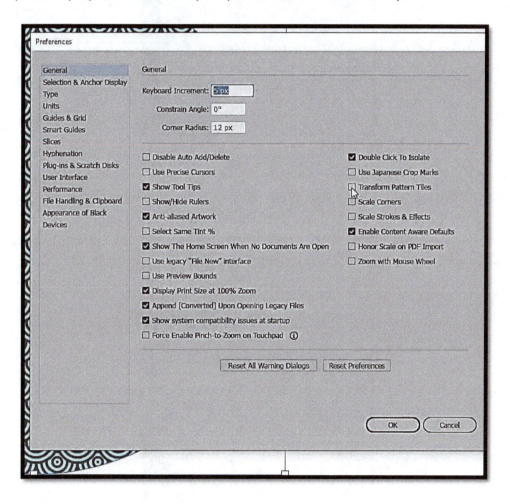

Another method that can be used to scale an applied pattern is to go to Object > Transform > Scale. Make sure that you uncheck the "Transform Objects" box so that the pattern will scale and not the entire object and then you can play with the horizontal and vertical values to scale the pattern or you can check the "Non-uniform" box if you are looking for a non-uniform scaling.

The third method that can be used to scale or even rotate an applied pattern is to go to Effect > Distort and transform > Transform. Play with these sliders to scale your pattern. Make sure that you enter identical values if you are looking for a uniform scaling. Again, uncheck the "Transform Objects" box to scale the pattern and not the entire object and you can play with that Angle spinner to rotate the pattern as you wish. Click OK to apply this effect.

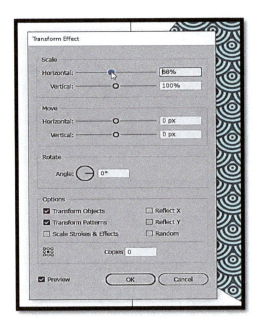

The nice thing about this technique is that you can always return to the Appearance panel where you can find this effect, open it, make some new changes, Click OK and the changes will be applied in an instant. Now that you know how patterns work feel free to use your imagination and create your own pattern designs.

Making blends

In this section, we're looking at using the Blender Tool in Illustrator. For this illustration, we are going to select a color to use then we're going to make a shape. It doesn't matter what shape you make, the shapes that you use for the Blend Tool can be the same or they can be different. Having made this one shape we are going to make a star and we'll give it a different color because then you'll see the full power of the Blend Tool as we work. Now we have a star that is roughly in alignment with the square.

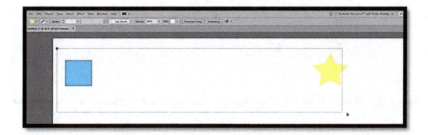

The Blend Tool

To use the Blend Tool you're going to select your shapes then go to Object > Blend > Make, and this makes a blend between the two shapes. What you see here may not be exactly what we see, it depends on whether you've used the Blend Tool previously or not because you might have it set to something different.

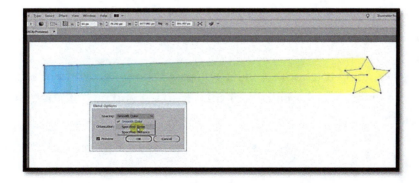

To see the settings select the blend, go to the Blend Tool, and click on it once to open the Blend options dialog. You'll need to turn on the preview so you can see what you're doing at the moment. We've got Smooth color and a smooth transition. This has gone smoothly from the first color to the second color. We've also transitioned from being a square to a star. We are now going to select "Specified steps" from this drop-down list and wind our steps back to say 6 because then it's going to be clear what's happening here.

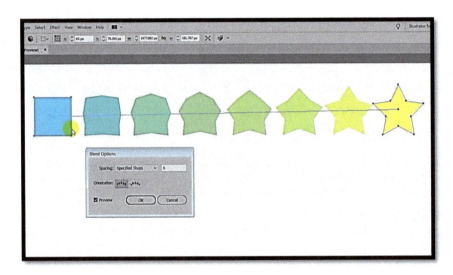

What Illustrator is doing is blending these shapes into each other; it's sort of morphing them as it goes so it's morphing the shape as well as the color. The next step is something else that you need. To be able to get these shapes out of the blend you're going to have to expand it. If we look here in the Layers palette we can see that we've got a bind in the Layers palette and the actual shapes aren't shapes yet we've got a star and the square and we've got the path along which the star and square are being blended. If we want these individual shapes we have to do something about that and that is to expand our blend.

Expand your blends

To do that we are going to choose Object > Blend, then go down to "Expand" and that just expands the blend into the individual shapes so we end up with one shape for each of these objects.

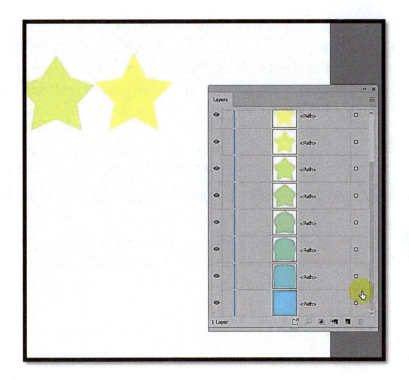

Blend around a shape

Moving forward, we are now going to show you how you can blend around a shape. We're going to start again with our star shape but let's make it a different color this time. We'll make it a sort of pink and drag out a small star. For our second object, we are just going to blend from one star to the other so we're going to settle for two pink stars.

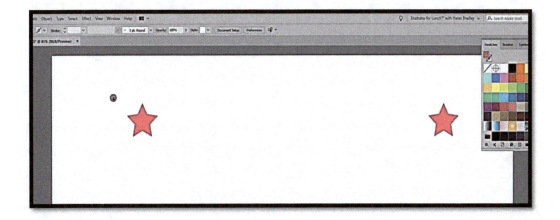

We'll select them, go to Object > Blend > Make. This time things aren't joining up the same way that they did last time. With our blend selected, we'll go back to the Blend Tool, and double-click on it to get the blend options. It's set to smooth color, we can do specified steps and if we take up the number of steps we can see how they blend into each other. This would probably be more apparent if we were transitioning from say a pink star to a blue star.

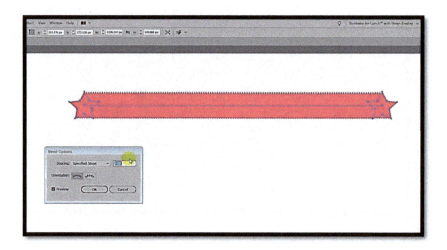

We are just going to reduce the number of steps that we've got on our blend so let's just take it down to 6. It's important to note that when you have specified 6 steps you're going to have eight stars so we've got one on either end and six in the middle. We are just going to click OK.

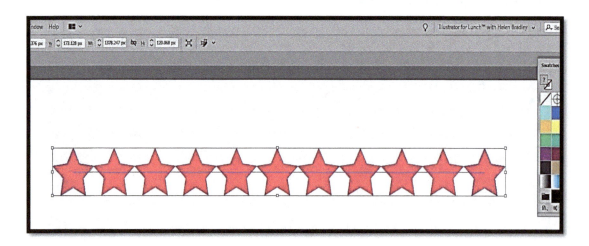

Now we want to put these stars around a circle and the way we do that is to draw our circle using the Ellipse Tool and we're just going to drag out a circle by holding the SHIFT key as we do that so that we are making a perfect circle for this.

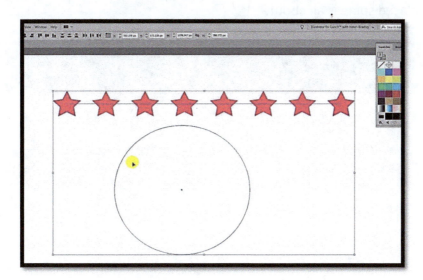

We can now go and apply the color as a stroke rather than a fill (it doesn't matter, we don't need a stroke or anything in this circle, we just need the circle to be made), then we're going to select both the blend and the circle. It doesn't matter what order they were created in, Illustrator is going to recognize which ones are Blend and which ones are circles. We're going to place the stars around the circle by going to Object > Blend and doing something called "Replacing spine."

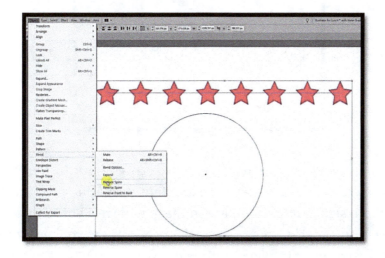

Let's just have a quick look at what these spines are about. When we click on this blend there's a line through it, and that is the spine. What we're saying to Illustrator is we know you've got a spine here but we'd like to replace this with the one we've got here so that's what this replaced spine is all about.

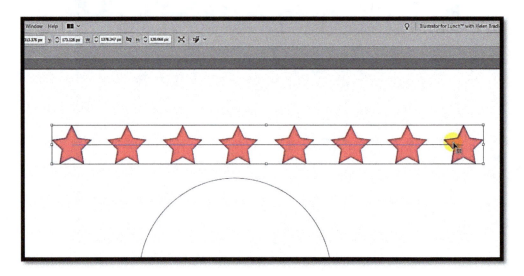

Back to our illustration, we'll select both shapes, go to Object > Blend > Replace spine, and what happens is that the stars are then placed around the circle.

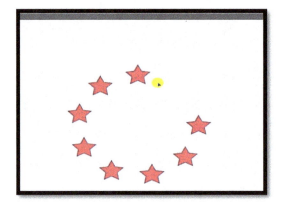

After selecting our blend with its new spine we can go back to the Blend Tool, turn preview on and we can increase or decrease the stars. Increasing and decreasing the stars is just making more stars but it's not filling in the gap. If we want to fill a gap in a closed shape, whether it be a circle, square, triangle, or whatever you're putting your blend around, you have to do what is called "Cutting this shape." You have to cut it and then it's going to work perfectly so we'll go over to the Scissors Tool and then we'll find the anchor point here. On a circle, there'll be an anchor point at the top, bottom, and either side. We are going to locate the one at the top and we're just going to click to cut it.

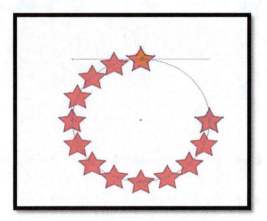

As soon as we cut it, the stars or the blend is now going all the way around the shape and of course, this is still a blend.

If we go to the Layers palette we're going to see that it is still a blend - we've got two stars and our spine this time instead of being aligned as fine as a circle but this is a blend. These are not individual shapes so they're also editable still.

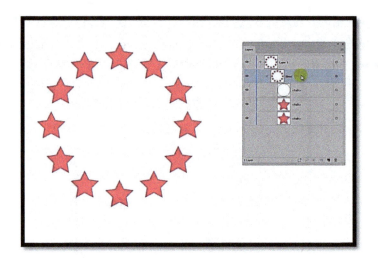

If we change the color of the other star to blue, we'll get a transition from the original pink star all the way around to a blue star. We can also double-click on the Blending options then go back to Specified steps and we can add more or fewer steps. While doing this, we can see that this is a live effect - these stars are changing color as they're being added to the design.

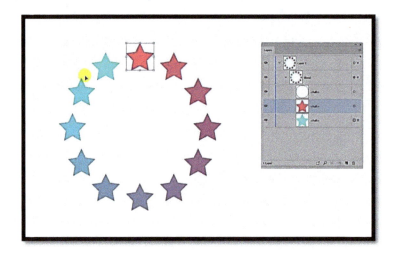

Once you're ready to settle on your design, once you're ready to bake this in and get individual stars then of course you're going to do exactly as we did before. You're going to select your blend and then expand that blend so now you have individual stars grouped in the Layers panel but each one of these is an individual star that you can then do other things with.

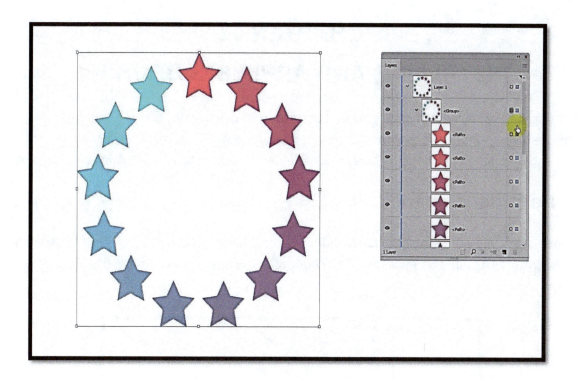

With that, you now know how to use the Blend Tool, make edits to the blend that you have created, replace a spine, and importantly how to break the objects out of a blend if you want to be able to deal with them independently.

Review Questions

1. How can you make your design look like it has light or dark areas using Adobe Illustrator?
2. Explain the process of creating patterns in Adobe Illustrator, and when this is useful.
3. What are the steps to make things look like they're smoothly blending in Adobe Illustrator and how can this make your design look better?

CHAPTER 12

INSTALLING AND APPLYING BRUSHES

Brushes are a really important part of Illustrator that can help you create complex designs more simply and can speed up your design creation process. In this chapter, we are going to show you the very basics of how to install, use, and save brushes in Adobe Illustrator.

The Brushes panel

Let's start with the Brushes panel, which is the place where you will find Brushes in Illustrator. To open this panel goes to Window > Brushes or you can use the F5 keyboard shortcut.

In this panel, you will find all five types of brushes that can be used in Illustrator. Calligraphy brushes and Scatter brushes are displayed in a square thumbnail box while Art brushes, Bristle brushes, and Pattern brushes are displayed in a horizontal rectangle.

Now let's see what all these buttons in the Brush panel do. Using the leftmost button, you can open other Brush libraries on your computer or you can save the brushes from your Brushes panel. You'll learn more about the settings at the end of the chapter after you learn how to create your own brushes. Let's move to the next button which can be used to easily open the Libraries panel. These next four buttons can be used to delete a brush from the brushes panel, create a new brush, adjust the settings of a brush that's already applied on a path, or simply remove a brush applied on a path. All these commands can also be found in the drop-down menu beside those options. In this menu you can change the view of your brushes in the Brushes panel, you can change what brushes to be shown in the Brushes panel or you can select the unused brushes to easily clean your Brushes panel.

Using a brush

Now that you know where to find brushes let's see how you can use one. Select the PaintBrush Tool from your toolbar or use the keyboard shortcut B, select a brush from the Brushes panel then simply click and drag to create your PaintBrush stroke.

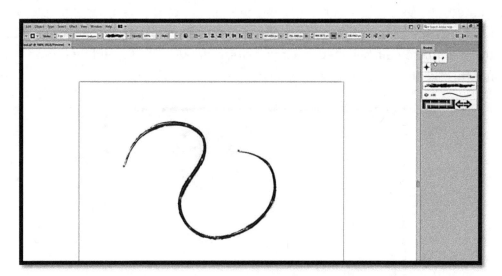

If you wish to apply a brush to an existing pad make sure that the pad is selected and then click the brush that you want to apply from the Brushes panel. Remove this pad if you have any, and double-click the PaintBrush Tool to open the window where you can check the settings that can be adjusted for this tool.

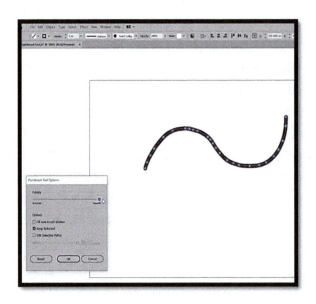

When you move the Fidelity slider to the left, the path that you are drawing is more accurate to your input. If you move the slider to the right, Illustrator adds a bit of smoothness to your drawn path. If you check the "Fill new brush strokes" box, the path, once created, also gets a fill color. If you change the fill color to red, for example, you can see when you draw the path and you finish creating it, you'll also get this red fill. If you want the path to remain selected once you finish drawing it all you have to do is make sure that this "keep selected" box is checked.

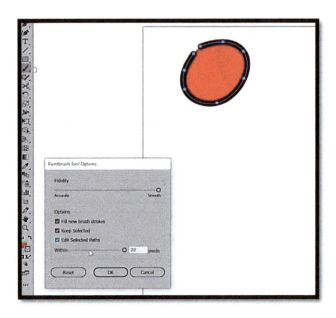

The third option will let you edit a path on top of a created path within the pixel range that you set with this slider. Let's say that you want to draw a line and you are not happy with the first attempt, all you have to do is draw a second one on top of the original one and as you release the button, this second attempt will replace the first one. Besides the settings from the PaintBrush Tool options window, you can press the SHIFT key before you start drawing a path to easily create straight and oblique pads or you can press the ALT/OPTION key after you start drawing a path to make sure that your path is closed after you release the mouse button.

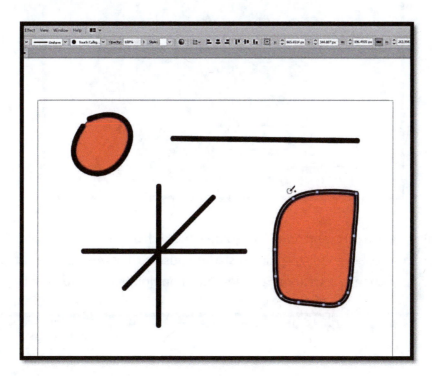

The different types of brushes

Now that you know where to find brushes and how to use them, let's learn more about the different types of brushes and how you can create your own brushes.

The Calligraphic brush

Let's start with the Calligraphic brush. To create a new brush simply clicks this "New brush" button. Make sure that the Calligraphic Brush box is checked and then click OK to open the window where you will set the settings of your new brush. Type in a name for this new brush, click OK and your new brush will show up in the Brushes panel.

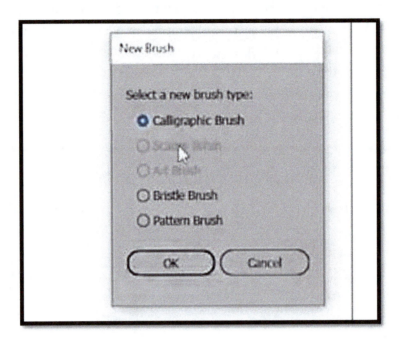

Select the PaintBrush Tool and your Calligraphic brush from the Brushes panel to draw a simple path. The color of a Calligraphic brush depends on the stroke color that you choose to select. You can change it to another color and then double-click your brush to edit it.

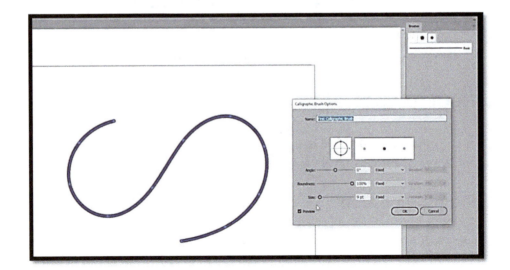

Make sure that you have the "Preview box" checked to notice the changes while you are editing the settings of your brush. By lowering this roundness value you can create a flatter brush and by using the angle and the size sliders you can adjust the angle of rotation and the diameter of your brush. Once you are done you can click OK and all the changes will be applied. Where the brush is used double-click your Calligraphic brush to increase the roundness to 100% and now let's see how the variables from these drop-down menus work. Most of these features are particularly useful if you are using a graphics tablet. Let's focus on the size settings to first exemplify this random variable. When the size is set to 10 and the variation is 5 the size range of the brush will go between 5 and 15. So when you are drawing paths using this brush you will get random sizes varying between 5 and 15. The other 5 variables can only be used if you own a graphics tablet.

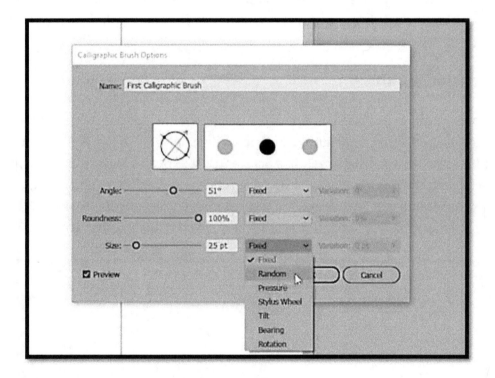

Let's start with pressure and see how it works. With the same size values the size range of the brush will go between 5 and 15 based on the pressure that you apply with the drawing stylus. When you are pressing harder the brush goes thicker and when you reduce the pressure the brush goes thinner. Let's get back to the Calligraphic brush and let's focus on the next variables.

151

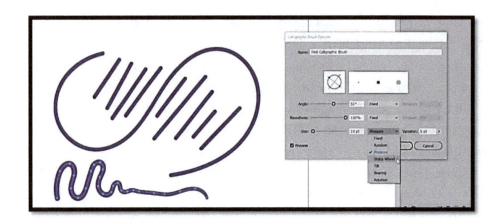

The Stylus wheel variable is created to be used with a brush pen that has a stylus wheel. The brush size will vary based on the manipulation of the stylus wheel. With these other three variables, the brush size will vary based on the tilt, the bearing, or the rotation of the pen's tip.

The Scatter brush

The second type of brush that you can create in Illustrator is the Scatter brush. To create one, you will need a shape or a group of shapes. Keep in mind that gradients and effects cannot be used when you are creating a Scatter brush. For this illustration, we will use a star. Select your star, click the "New brush" button, check the Scatter Brush box, and then click OK to open the window where you will set the settings of your new brush. Enter a name click, OK and your new Scatter brush will show up in the Brushes panel.

Select the PaintBrush Tool from your toolbar to draw a simple path and then double-click your Scatter brush to better understand all these settings. Make sure that you have the Preview enabled to notice all the changes as you make them. Using these sliders here, you can set the size, spacing, scatter, and rotation of the Brush elements. These values are always in relation to the original shape that you choose to use for your Scatter brush. When you choose a random size you can use these two sliders to specify a range within which the size of the Brush elements should vary. As with the other brushes, you will need a graphics tablet to use one of these variations. From the "Rotation relative to" drop-down menu, You can set the angle of rotation for the Brush elements relative to the page or relative to the path.

Let's keep it relative to the page. The color of a Scatter brush depends on the stroke color that you choose to select and the colorization method that you set from this menu. The same rules apply to Art Brushes and Pattern Brushes. Let's focus on the colorization method and open this drop-down menu. When you select Tints, black is replaced with the stroke color. Colors that are not black are replaced with tints of the stroke color and white doesn't change. Selecting Tints and Shades will replace the existing colors with tints and shades of the stroke color. Black and white does not change. Selecting Hue shift will replace the existing colors with the stroke color based on this key color.

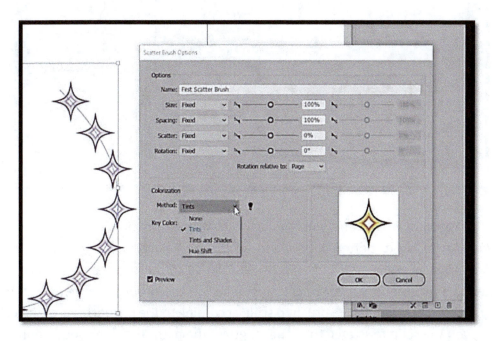

By default, the most present color from your brush is said to be the key color. To change this key color just click the Eyedropper icon and click the color that you want to be set as key from the preview. The sections from the brush that use the key color will be replaced with the stroke color, and the other colors will be replaced with variations of the stroke color; again, black and white do not change. Another way to understand better how these colorization methods work is to always click these Tips button

Art brush

The third type of brush that you can create in Illustrator is the Art brush. As with the other brushes, remember that gradients and effects cannot be used when you are saving an Art brush. Click the "New brush" button, check the Art brush box, and then click OK to open this window where you will be able to set the settings of your new brush. Change the name, click OK and your new Art brush will show up in the Brushes panel.

Select the PaintBrush Tool and your Art brush to draw a simple path and then double-click your Art brush to better understand all these settings. Using the slider you can increase or decrease the width of your brush relative to the original shape and as with Calligraphic brushes and Scatter brushes you can use the drop-down menu for the Pen tablet variables. You can set the brush to scale according to the proportions of the original shape or you can set it to stretch to fit the length of the path. The third option here allows you to set a specific section of the brush that should stretch. If you move the guide to the middle, the section on the right will stretch while the one on the left will remain as it is in its original shape. Check "Stretch to fit," increases the width to 100 percent, and then focuses on the Direction option. Using these arrow buttons you can set the orientation of the brush in relation to the path. The blue arrow allows you to better understand how the brush is applied on the path. When it comes to colorization the settings for Art brushes are the same as the settings for Scatter brushes. With these bottom options, you can easily flip your brush along the pad, across the pad or you can fix this unwanted overlap using the second Overlap button.

The Bristle brush

The fourth type of brush that you can create in Illustrator is the Bristle brush. To create one, simply click the "New brush" button, check the Bristle brush box, and then click OK to open the window where you will set the settings of your new brush. As with the other brushes, you can change the name, click OK and your new Bristle brush will show up in the Brushes panel.

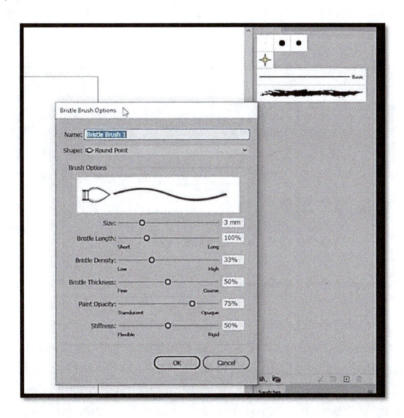

Select the PaintBrush Tool to draw a simple pad using your Bristle brush and then double-click it to have a closer look at all the settings. From the Shapes drop-down menu you can select the style of the brush tip, these options are pretty straightforward and give you endless possibilities to create any Bristle brush that you may need. You can adjust the brush size, the length of the bristles, the density of the bristles which is calculated based on the values that you set for the first two options, the thickness of the bristles, the opacity of the used paint, and the rigidness of the bristles. When you are done, click OK. Before we move on you should know that the color of a bristle brush depends on the straw color that you choose to select.

The Pattern brush

The last type of brush that you can create in Illustrator is a Pattern brush. As with the other brushes, gradients, and effects cannot be used when you are saving a pattern brush. Select the shapes you want, click the "New brush" button, check the Pattern brush box, and then click OK to open the window where you will be able to set the settings of your new Pattern brush. Type in a name, click OK and your new Pattern brush will show up in the Brushes panel.

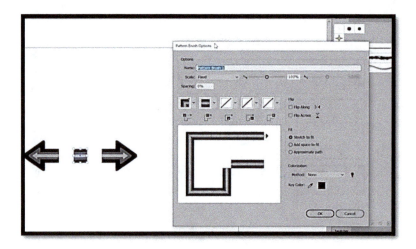

Select the PaintBrush Tool to draw a simple path using your Pattern brush and then double-click it to have a closer look at all these options here. Make sure that you have the Preview box checked and let's focus on the scale settings. Using this slider, you can adjust the width of the brush relative to the original shape that you choose to use for your pattern brush. Bring it back to 100 percent and as with the other brushes, from the Scale

156

drop-down menu, you can access the tablet variables. You can add some space between the tiles that make up your Pattern brush, you can flip your Pattern brush along the pad or across the pad, and with these Fit options you are setting the behavior of the tiles that make up your Pattern brush. "Stretch to fit" will stretch the tiles to fit the length of the entire pad. "Add space to fit" will add space between the tiles and the size of the tiles will not change. "Approximate path" will approximate the closest path that is needed to perfectly fit the tiles without affecting the size of the tiles.

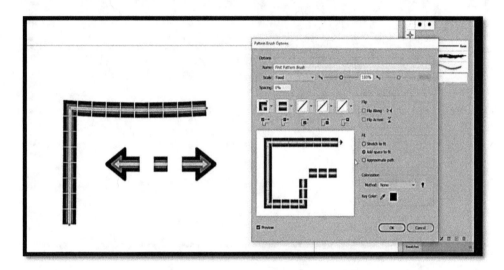

When it comes to colorization, the settings for Pattern brushes are the same as the settings for Art brushes and scatter brushes. By using these tile buttons you are setting the appearance for specific sections from a Pattern brush. The main elements that you use to save your Pattern brush are used for this side tile and Illustrator generates for you tiles for the corners of a Pattern brush. You can select them from the drop-down menu. For the start tile and the end tile, you have to create your own designs.

How to create and apply tiles to a Pattern brush

Let's show you how you can create your own tiles and how you can apply them to a Pattern brush. Select the elements you want to use and simply drag them inside the Swatches panel to save them as patterns. Get back to the Brushes panel and double-click your Pattern brush. From the start tile select "New pattern Swatch 1," and from the end tile select "New pattern Swatch 2." Click ok to apply the changes.

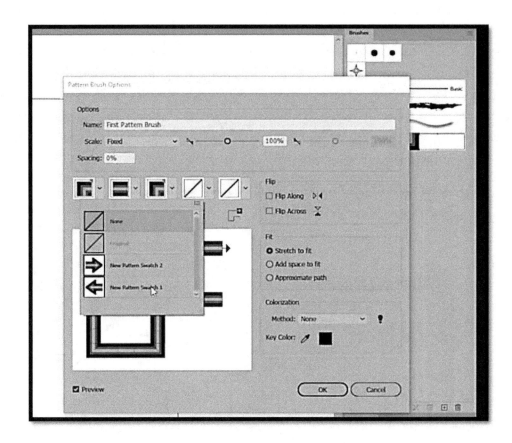

Select the PaintBrush Tool and draw some smooth arrows, remember that you can always change the colorization to Tints and you can easily change the color of your arrow. In some cases, the corner tiles that Illustrator generates for your Pattern brush might not look as you wish and in this case, you will have to create your own corner tiles. Throughout this chapter, we kept mentioning that you cannot use gradients for brushes but keep in mind that you can use blends; you can create a blend that looks like a gradient and create a brush out of it.

Loading your Brushes

When you want to load a set of brushes, simply double-click the Illustrator document and focus on the Brushes panel where you will notice that your brushes are already loaded and ready to use. If you can't see this panel all you have to do is go to Window in the menu bar and select Brushes.

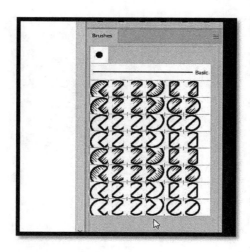

Applying your brush

Now that you have your brushes let's see how easy it can be to apply one. Select the Ellipse Tool from your toolbar, create a simple path, and select a brush from the Brushes panel that you want to apply on your path. Much more commonly you can use the PaintBrush Tool to check how your brush handles a variety of angles and curved paths.

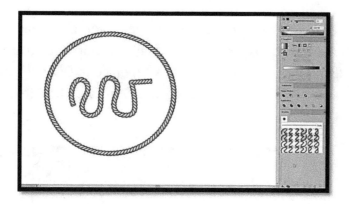

Saving your brush

Now let's say that you'll only need the top four brushes, remove the button for brushes and to use these brushes in another document you'll have to save them. To do this, all you have to do is click the first button in the bottom right corner and go to 'Save brushes" or you can open the flier menu from the Brushes panel and go to "Save brush library."

You can save your brushes in the Preset folder or you can select a different one (for this illustration we'll save them in the Preset folder), type in a name for your new set of brushes, and click Save.

Accessing your saved brushes

If you saved your brushes in the Preset folder, when you click that first button in the bottom right corner and go to User Defined you will find your set of brushes. Alternatively, you can open the flyout menu from the Brushes panel, go to Open brush library and User Defined and again you will find your set of brushes. Simply click on it and you will get the panel with your set of brushes.

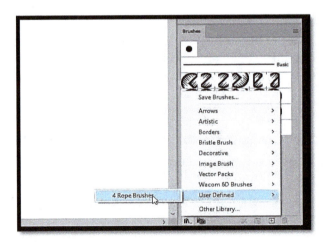

When you choose to save your brushes in a different folder you can access them by going to "Other Library." You have the same command in the menu of the Brushes panel.

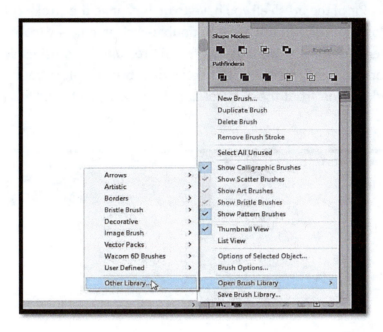

How you organize your brushes is entirely up to you. Besides your saved brushes you'll notice some Preset collections of brushes that come with Illustrator. You can load any of these brush libraries with a simple click. Keep in mind that you can use these arrow buttons to easily navigate between the Preset brush libraries and when you find the brush that you need just click it to apply it on the selected path.

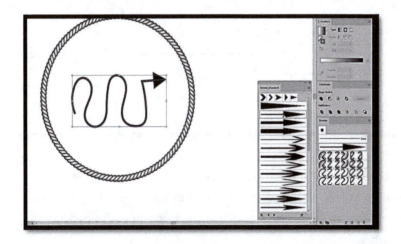

Changing the color of a brush

To change the color of the brush all you have to do is change the stroke color. You can do it from the Color panel or you can do it by double-clicking on the Stroke color wheel in the toolbar, then pick a color and click OK. For more complex brushes you can use the "Recolor artwork" option to change the color of a brush. Select your path, click the Recolor Artwork button from the Control panel, or go to Edit > Edit Colors > Recolor artwork.

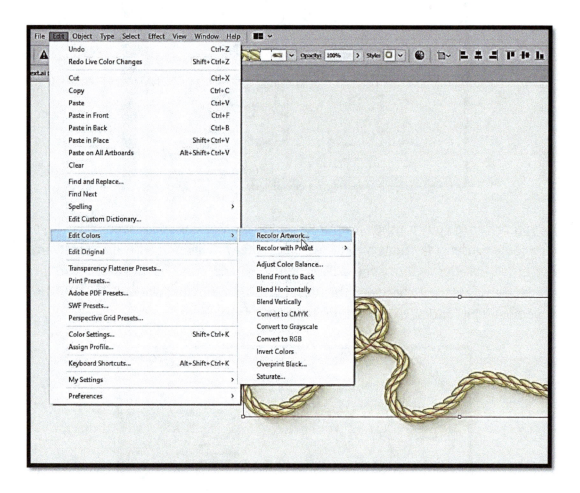

Click the Advanced Options button to get access to all the settings of the "Recolor artwork" option and using these color buttons here you can change each color one by one or you can switch to the Edit mode and use these color handles to change all the colors of the brush at once.

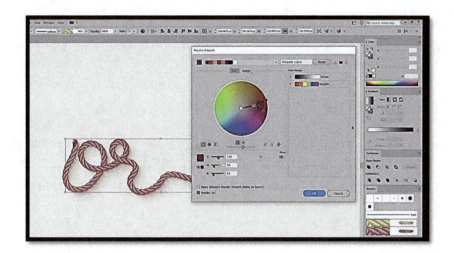

Changing the size of your brush

To change the size of a brush all you have to do is adjust the Stroke weight from the Control panel.

Applying gradients on brushes

You should know that it is not possible to apply gradients on Illustrator brushes. If you need to do this you will have to expand your brush. Before you expand the brush, first remove the fill color (if any) and then go to Object > Expand Appearance. Unite the resulting group of shapes using the first button from the Pathfinder panel and then fill your shape with a radial gradient.

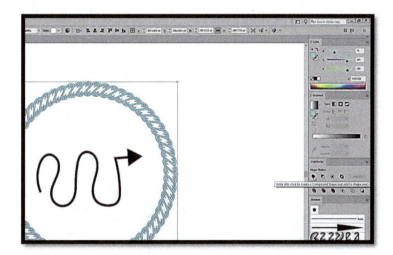

You can move this gradient slider around eighty percent, changes the color mode to RGB, and select your color. Then select the other gradient slider, again change the Color mode to RGB, and select a darker color.

Editing a certain instance of the brush

One more tip before we conclude this chapter is that you can edit a certain instance of the brush without affecting the other strokes using the Stroke Options button. Make the change that you want, click OK and you can see that only the selected path gets the edit.

Review Questions

1. How do you install brushes in Adobe Illustrator, and why is this helpful for making your artwork better?
2. Explain how to use brushes on your artwork in Adobe Illustrator, and give examples of how different brushes can change the way it looks.
3. Are there any important things to remember when using brushes in Adobe Illustrator?

CHAPTER 13
APPLYING EFFECTS

In this chapter, we are going to be explaining every effect of Adobe Illustrator. Before we proceed, some things you have to know are:

- Effects follow a non-destructive workflow, which means any changes they make are reversible - you can always edit, hide, or delete them.
- Effects interact with each other, so you can stack multiple effects on a single object for increasingly complex visuals.
- Effects and the Appearance Panel work together. You can use the panel to view, edit, hide, delete, and move effects on any object.

Exploring the various effects

3D and Materials effect

The 3D and Materials effect has so many customization options that it has its own panel.

There are 3 different tabs on the 3D effect: Object, Materials, and Lighting.

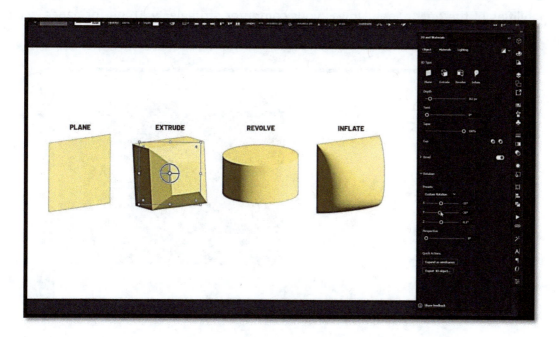

- **The Object tab has the most important setting:** the 3D Type. This is where you can define and customize the shape of your 3D object, and each 3D type has its own set of options for customization. Below the 3D Type section, you can add and customize bevels and at the bottom, you can rotate the object and adjust the camera's perspective.
- On the Materials tab, you can apply different materials and textures to the object. You have the default material, very basic and without any textures, and a selection of more complex and realistic materials from Adobe Substance. At the bottom, you can customize the properties of the materials and change how they look.
- Lastly, on the Lighting tab, you can add and customize light sources. You can change the light settings using the sliders, or select one of the presets. There's a list of all the light sources in the scene, and you can add new ones by clicking on the "Add Light" button. At the very bottom, you can turn on shadows, which makes the object way more realistic. On the top right corner of the panel, you can turn on rendering or open the render settings to fine-tune it.

3D Classic

The classic 3D effect is a legacy effect which got replaced by the new 3D and Materials effect. You can still use it to simulate 3D vectors, but it doesn't have any of the ray tracing capabilities of the new panel. Unless your computer struggles with performance, we'd recommend using the new 3D effect over this one.

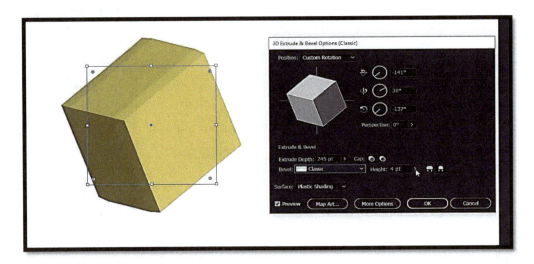

Convert-to-Shape effect

The "Convert to Shape" effect transforms the selected object into one of three shapes: rectangle, rounded rectangle, or ellipse. The shape size can be either absolute, which means the final shape will have that exact size, or relative, which means the final shape will add extra width and height to the original object.

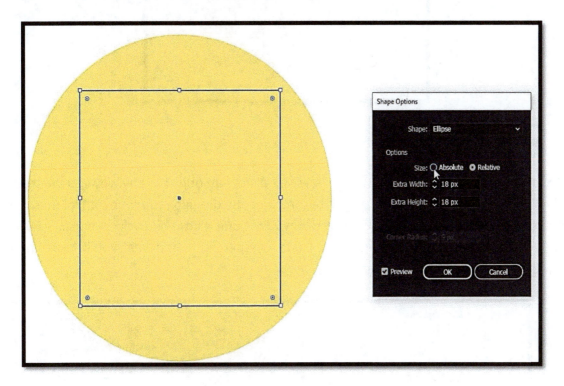

This effect is not particularly useful on its own. However, when combined with other effects or text, it can produce interesting results. For example, you can add a new fill to a text object and use the "Convert to Shape" effect to create a box behind the text that automatically scales as you type.

Crop Marks effect

The Crop Marks effect adds four crop marks on the corners of the selected object. Crop marks indicate where you want the printed paper to be cut.

Free Distort effect

The Free Distort effect allows you to skew and distort an object in any way you want. On the Effects window, you can manipulate the object by dragging the four control points in the corners. It is similar to the Free Transform Tool, but a little bit trickier to use. Still, it's a useful non-destructive alternative to add perspective - and yes, you'll hear "non-destructive" a lot in this chapter.

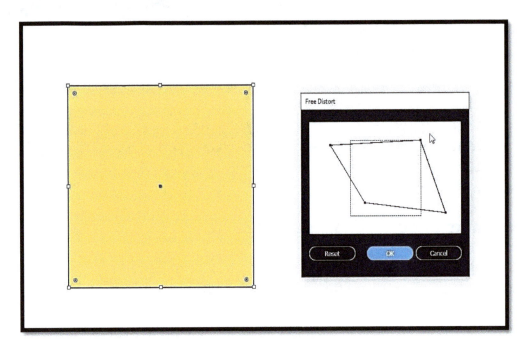

This is also the perfect opportunity to talk about the stacking order of effects in the Appearance Panel. The Appearance Panel displays all the elements that make up an object, such as fills, strokes, opacity, and effects, and organizes them in layers. Changing the order of these layers can change the final look of the object. Let's take a square as an example. It currently has two layers: a fill and a stroke. If we add a Free Distort effect, it will appear at the bottom of the stack and distort the object.

We can also add a Drop Shadow effect which we'll talk about later in this chapter. It appears once again at the bottom of the stack and adds a shadow that matches the shape of the object after the distortion.

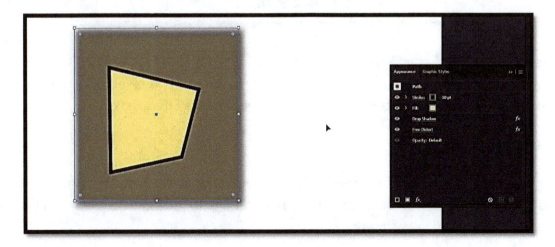

But what if we move the shadow above the distortion? The result is quite weird, but it makes sense if we think about it - we're first applying the shadow to the object, which is a square, and only then distorting it. Here's another cool thing: we can also apply effects to individual fills or strokes. For example, if we drag the Free Distort effect inside the Fill layer, only the Fill will be distorted while the stroke remains a square. Similarly, if we move it inside the stroke layer, only the stroke will be distorted. The same is true for the Drop Shadow effect, which only affects the stroke when we move it inside the stroke layer. So many different looks with just two effects, right?

Pucker & Bloat effect

The Pucker & Bloat effect moves the anchor points towards or away from the center of the object. Dragging the slider to the left pushes the anchor points outwards, making the object pointy. Dragging it to the right, pushes the anchor points inwards, making the object round.

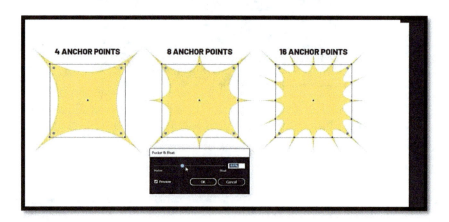

Pucker is very good at making sparkles and stars, while Bloat is perfect for making cute flowers. Since this effect manipulates anchor points, even if two objects look the same, the number of anchor points they have will change how the effect looks.

The Roughen effect

The Roughen effect adds a random texture to strokes and fills, creating a hand-drawn look. This is a cool effect for when you need something to look more natural and hand-made, or just to add visual interest.

170

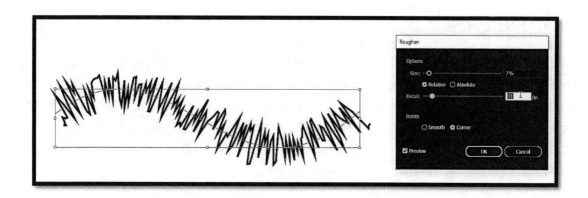

There are two main controls on the effect: size and detail, and the easiest way to understand them are by looking at a simple line. Size adds distortion away from the original path, while detail adds distortion along the path. If you look at a straight line, you can also think of them as vertical distortion and horizontal distortion. You also have the option to use relative or absolute size. Relative uses a percentage, while Absolute uses a fixed number. This affects how the effect scales - with relative size, the effect scales up or down with the object. With absolute size, the effect stays the same.

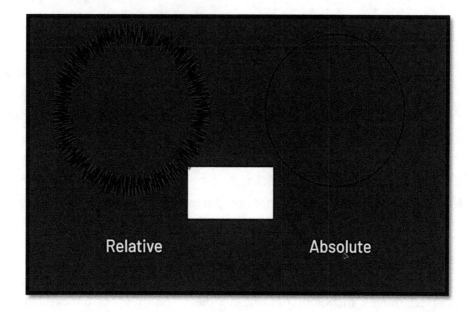

At the bottom, you can also choose if you want the distortion to have smooth curves or sharp corners. Different from the Pucker & Bloat effect, Roughen is not anchor point dependent, so even a straight line with only two anchor points will be distorted.

Transform effect

The Transform effect allows you to apply basic transformations to the object, like scale, rotation, and position. For scale and position, you can change vertical and horizontal parameters independently. In the Options section, you can apply the effect only to the object, to the pattern, or both, as well as reflect and apply the transformation randomly. This is one of those effects that look simple on the surface but offer you a wide array of possibilities to create very complex things.

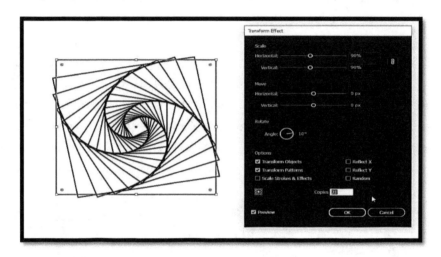

At the very bottom of the Effects window you have the option to create copies, and the cool thing is that every copy will stack another instance of the effect. So if you're rotating 10 degrees and scaling down 10 percent, each subsequent copy you add will be rotated another 10 degrees and scaled down another 10 percent, allowing you to create beautiful geometric patterns with just a few clicks. Just be very careful when making copies, because this effect can have a huge impact on performance depending on how complex the object is and how many copies you're making.

Tweak effect

The Tweak effect moves anchor points and handles randomly, for a more chaotic look. It's a very odd effect and even though it is random, you do have sliders to control how much distortion you want, either vertically or horizontally, and if you want to use relative or absolute values.

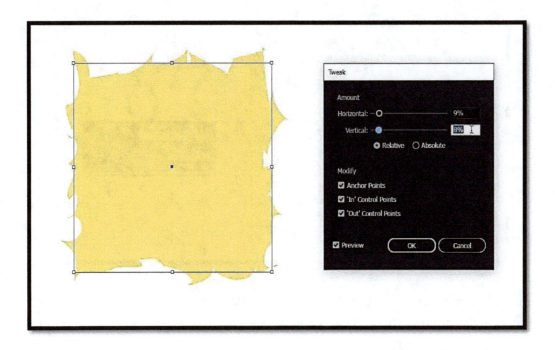

Basically, when you apply the effect it defines a random ratio between each anchor point and handle, so even if you increase the distortion, the ratio between them stays the same. It's worth noting that every time you apply the effect, it generates a new random seed, so even if you have multiple objects with the same anchor points, each one will look different. This effect works similarly to the Roughen effect, but it is anchor point dependent, so just like Pucker & Bloat, the number of anchor points and where they are placed will influence how the Tweak effect looks. At the bottom of the Effects window, you'll also find options to modify anchor points or handles, both in and out. However, illustrator calls them "Control points" here for some reason. Leaving anchor points unchecked keeps all the anchor points in place, and just moves the handles, and vice versa. To sum it up, it is good if you want to create random scribbles or shapes that look wild.

Twist effect

The best way to explain the Twist effect is to imagine that you are placing the object inside a vortex. That's all it does. This effect only has one control, which is the angle, and the more you turn it up, the more twisted the object becomes.

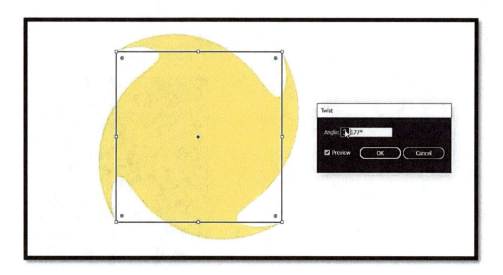

You may see some uses for it, but if you set the angle to a high value, objects start looking the same. It also creates some imperfections along the curves so keep that in mind.

ZigZag effect

The ZigZag effect works the same as the Roughen Effect, but instead of random distortion, it distorts in a zig-zag pattern. Other than that, all controls are the same. Size distorts vertically away from the path, and segments distort horizontally along the path. Relative and Absolute switch between percentages and fixed numbers, and at the bottom you can leave the zig-zag sharp or rounded.

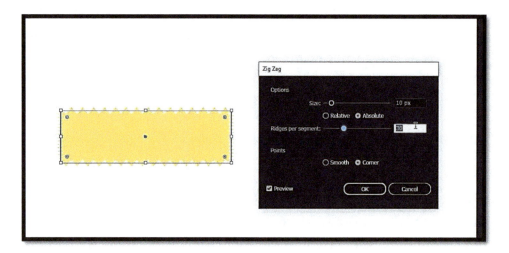

The downside to this effect is that it adds a fixed number of ridges per segment of the path, so unless your object has every segment the same size, this effect doesn't look interesting. The way around this problem is to add more anchor points, but that really shouldn't be the way it works. Zig Zag is a cool effect. Despite the limitations, it works great to great badges and stamps or to just add some detail to a simple shape.

Offset Path effect

The Offset Path effect is pretty self-explanatory. When applied, it offsets the path by a specific amount, either inwards or outwards. On the Effects window, there are three parameters. First, you can input how much the path will be offset, and it's worth noting you can also input negative values to offset inwards. Then you can choose the corner type. There's Miter, Round, and Bevel. Lastly, you can define a limit for the miter join, which is an angle threshold for the sharp corner to turn into a miter.

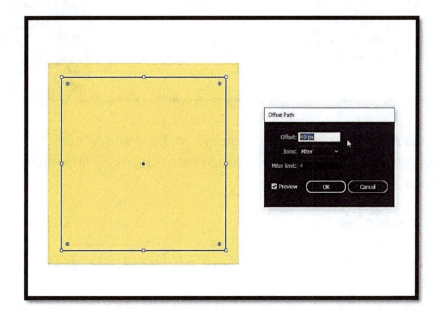

The Offset Path effect is particularly useful in workflows where you're stacking multiple fills, strokes, and effects, and you might need a layer to be bigger than the rest so you can see it. You could also use the Transform effect to increase the size of a layer, and for some shapes that might work, but Transform will just scale the object up, while Offset Path will enlarge the path by a consistent amount throughout the object.

Outline Object effect

The Outline Object effect is mostly used to add strokes to images. If you ever tried to add an outline to an image in Illustrator, you know it is not possible. However, if you select the stroke in the Appearance panel and add the Outline Object effect, the stroke shows up.

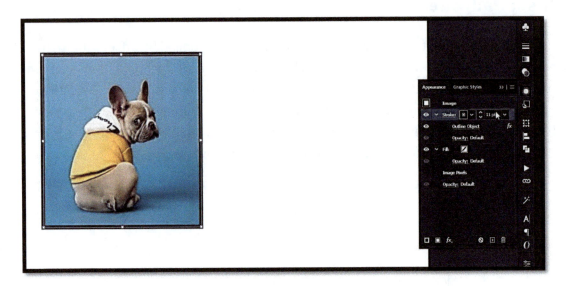

You can also use this effect to show a more precise bounding box around text objects. However, you also need to open the Preferences Menu and toggle "Use Preview Bounds." This makes such a huge difference.

Outline Stroke effect

The Outline Stroke effect, on the other hand, is much more useful and easy to understand. This effect transforms the stroke into a filled object; it works just like using the Expand option in the Object Menu. This can severely change how effects are applied to the object. Effects like Roughen produce quite distinct outcomes depending on whether Outline Stroke is applied or not. Without Outline Stroke, the Roughen effect distorts the original path along which the stroke runs. When Outline Stroke is applied, the stroke turns into a rectangle, so the Roughen effect distorts the outer edges of the stroke and not the original path.

Pathfinder effect

The Pathfinder effect is a non-destructive way to combine shapes using the Boolean operations from the Pathfinder panel. To apply this effect, you need to group at least two objects. Once you have the group selected, go to the Effects menu and choose the operation you want. If you don't get it right the first time, you can access more options by opening the Effects window through the Appearance panel. At the top of the window, you'll find a drop-down menu with all available operations.

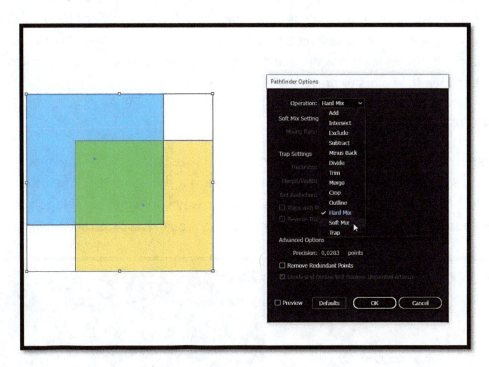

Most of them combine the shapes in some way, while the last three deal with color, which we will discuss shortly. Pathfinder operations are too many and too complex to explain so we recommend you just scroll through them until you get the result you want. Some are very easy to understand, like Intersect, which deletes everything but the parts that are overlapping, or Exclude, which does the opposite.

As for the last three options:

- First, you have "Hard Mix." This operation compares the color channels (RGB or CMYK) of both objects and selects the darkest value for each channel to create a new color. If we are using blue and yellow, for example, the darkest values are 56 for red, 189 for green, and 88 for blue. Comparing the resulting green with the green from the Hard Mix operation, we can see that it is a perfect match.

- Soft Mix, on the other hand, despite the similar name, is not exactly the opposite of Hard Mix. Soft Mix makes the underlying colors visible through the overlapping artwork. In practical terms, it is making the yellow object transparent, but only where the two objects overlap. If you expand the objects through the Object menu, you'll see that both Hard Mix and Soft Mix also divide the objects into their component faces.

- Finally, we have Trap, which is a bit more complex and may not be so commonly used. When two overlapping colors are printed using the CMYK color mode, they can sometimes leave a white gap between them. Trapping creates a small overlap between the colors to prevent this from happening.

Rasterize effect

The Rasterize effect is a non-destructive way to Rasterize objects. Rasterize means to turn into a raster image, an image made out of pixels, like a JPEG or a PNG. The other option is to select Rasterize on the Object menu, but this way you won't be able to toggle the rasterization on and off or continue to edit the vector object. It'll become an image.

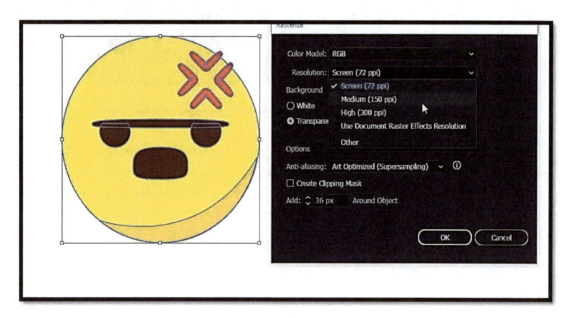

With the Rasterize effect, you can preview the object rasterized, while still maintaining the ability to edit it and even apply other effects. On the Effects window, at the very top, you can choose the color model and resolution. Usually, you'll use 72 for digital and 150 or 300 for printing. On the background section, you can choose to leave it transparent or fill it with white. On the Options section, you can turn on anti-aliasing, either optimized for art or text. Anti-aliasing is a technique to smooth out rough edges and reduce pixelation by blending colors along the edges of objects. Finally, you can offset the outer bounds of the image by how many pixels you input here, and check the "Create Clipping Mask" box to automatically create a clipping mask using the shape of the vector itself.

Drop Shadow effect

Drop Shadow is perhaps the most used effect in Illustrator. It's a pretty simple and easy-to-understand effect, but that doesn't mean there aren't a few cool things about it. Drop Shadow is very self-explanatory - it adds a shadow behind the object. You can define the opacity of the shadow, the X and Y position, and the blur, which is basically how soft the shadow is. At the bottom, you can choose between a specific color and a darkness value. The darkness option uses the color of the object itself and gradually adds black to it, creating a shadow that has a little bit of the object's color in it - in our case, a shadow that is a little bit yellow, and not straight up black. This looks way more realistic.

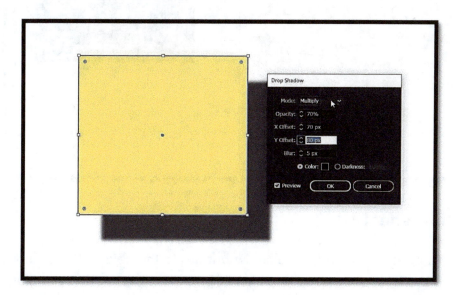

You can also change the blending mode of the effect. Blending modes are ways to blend a color with everything that's below it. By default, the effect comes with the multiply effect selected, which darkens what's below but if you select the Screen blending mode and choose a brighter color, you can turn the drop shadow into a glow effect. The Drop Shadow effect is also the first raster effect on the list, which means that the effect itself is a raster image and not a vector. You can see that by zooming into the shadow to see the pixels showing up. This happens with every effect that requires some sort of blur. The resolution of raster effects is selected when you create a new document. However, if you want to change the resolution later, you can do it by going to the Effects menu and choosing Document > Raster Effects Settings.

Feather effect

If you're familiar with Photoshop, you already know what Feather does. If not, don't worry its super simple: the Feather effect blurs the edges of the object in a soft fade to transparent.

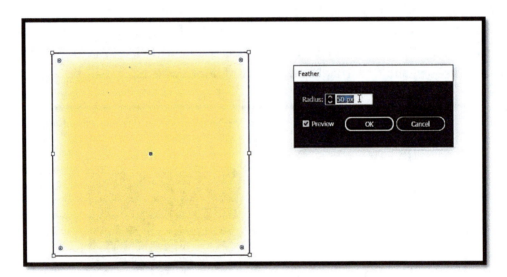

Inner Glow effect

The Inner Glow effect is like Drop Shadow but inside the object. There's not much to control in this effect - you can choose blending mode, color, opacity, and blur, and you already know how all of this works from the Drop Shadow effect. At the bottom, you have the Options Center and Edge, and toggling between them inverts the starting point of the glow. If you set the blending mode to multiply and pick a dark color, you can also use this effect as an inner shadow.

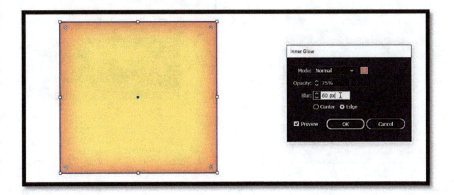

Outer Glow effect

If Inner Glow was like Drop Shadow, Outer Glow is Drop Shadow, just without the X and Y position. It's Drop Shadow with position set to 0. Absolutely the same effect, no difference at all.

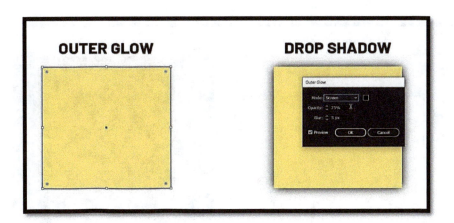

Round Corners effect

The Round Corners effect lost a bit of its use with the introduction of live corners, but it's still a great way to round corners in a non-destructive way. The effect is as simple as it gets: it rounds sharp corners. You have one option in the Effects window, which is the radius of the roundness.

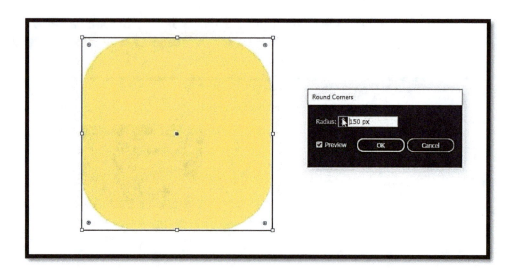

Scribble effect

Scribble is such a fun little effect. It's the easiest way to turn your design into a sketch or even a child drawing. The effect turns any fill or stroke into scribbles, and there are a lot of customization options.

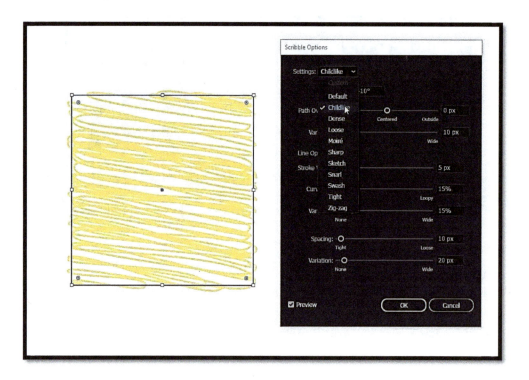

First, we have a drop-down menu with a ton of presets. Some are more contained, some are more chaotic. They're a great place to start customizing the effect. Then, we can choose the angle at which the scribbles go, as well as the Path Overlap. This is an Offset Path inside the Scribble effect.

If you drag the slider to the left, it offsets the scribbles inwards, and if you drag it to the right, it offsets outwards. Below, there is a Variation control that adds some randomness to Path Overlap. If you set Variation to 5 pixels, for example, the value you selected in Path Overlap will randomly fluctuate between -5 and +5 for every line of the scribble, giving it a more loose, natural, and hand-drawn look.

Then, we have some line options. You can change the stroke width, curviness, and spacing. Stroke width is self-explanatory, and while it, unfortunately, doesn't have a variation control, curviness and spacing do. Curviness controls the behavior of the scribble at the end of each stroke. If set to angular, the end of the stroke will be a sharp corner, and dragging the slider to the right adds curviness, making it, again, more loose and natural. Variation will work the same way as previously explained, adding randomness.

You can keep curviness at 0 and then add a little bit of variation. Spacing controls the space in between each stroke of the scribble, from tight to loose. This severely affects performance, since a tighter scribble will have more lines drawn. Be careful not to drag this slider to the left, as it will draw so many lines that Illustrator might crash. It's worth mentioning that you can apply separate Scribble effects on the fill and the stroke through the Appearance Panel, since the settings that look good on the fill, might not on the stroke.

SVG Filters

SVG Filters are effects aimed at web design. SVG effects differ from their bitmap counterparts in that they are XML-based and resolution-independent. In fact, an SVG effect is nothing more than a series of XML properties that describe various mathematical operations. The resulting effect is rendered to the target object instead of the source graphic.

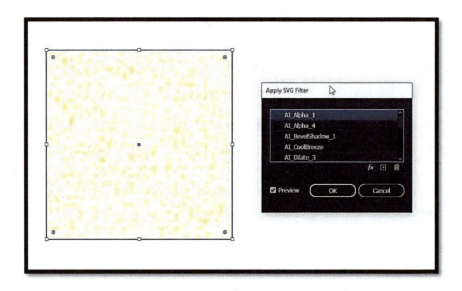

Illustrator comes with a list of default, pre-installed filters, which you can access by clicking on the effect on the Appearance Panel. On the Effects window, you can access the XML code by clicking on the FX button, or write your own code and create your own filters by clicking on the plus button.

Warp effect

Warp is, once again, a non-destructive way to apply something from the Object menu - this time, an Envelope Distort with Warp. The Warp effect uses a mesh to distort the object in many different ways, which can be selected either through the Effects menu or on the Effects window itself.

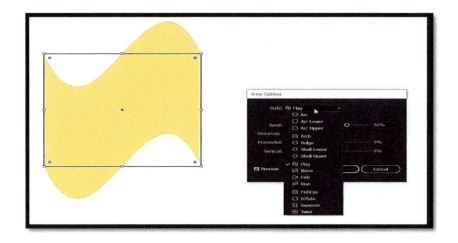

After selecting the style you want for the distortion, you can use the Bend slider to change the amount of distortion you want to apply. Using negative values will invert the mesh, distorting the object in the opposite direction. You can also apply the bend to the object either horizontally or vertically. In the distortion section, you can add perspective to the bend, either horizontally or vertically.

Review Questions

1. What are 5 cool effects that you can put on your artwork in Adobe Illustrator, and how do they make it look better?
2. Explain how to add shadows, 3D effects, and distortions to your artwork in Adobe Illustrator, and explain how to adjust them.
3. Give examples of how you can use effects to create a certain feeling or style in your artwork.

CHAPTER 14

GOING PRO WITH ILLUSTRATOR

In this chapter, we are going to show you all that you need to know about Illustrator's Appearance and Graphics Styles panels. After that, we will quickly look at the Creative Cloud library.

The Appearance Panel and Graphic Styles

The Appearance panel along with the Graphics Styles panel is one of the most important features in Illustrator and once you master these panels your workflow will increase greatly.

The Appearance panel

To open it you can either go to Window in the menu bar or select Appearance or you can use the SHIFT and F6 keyboard shortcut. By default, you will get a black stroke and a white field.

In the top left corner, you can find a thumbnail that represents the existing Appearance settings. If you can't see it you need to open the menu and select "Show thumbnail." If you wish to hide that thumbnail you need to select "Hide thumbnail" from this menu. You can simply click and drag it onto an object from your design whenever you wish to apply the existing Appearance settings to that object.

Next to the thumbnail, there's the title bar. In the beginning, this can be useful to know exactly the type of object that you have selected. It can be a path type, a group, or even a layer and it also lets you know if a graphic style is applied. Back to the slider bar you need to select it whenever you wish to be sure that an effect that you're about to add gets applied on the entire object, not just a particular fill or stroke from your design. Finally, you have the opacity bar. Click this opacity text to open the transparency flyout panel which can be used to adjust the opacity or the blending mode settings for the object that you have selected. Again, these changes will affect the entire object, not just a particular fill or stroke from your design.

Graphic Styles

One method you can save the Appearance settings is as a Graphic Style and then use that graphic style to easily apply the same attributes to other objects. You can open the Graphic Styles panel by going to Window > Graphic Styles or you can use the SHIFT+F5 keyboard shortcut. To save a new graphic style all you have to do is click the "New Graphic Style" button to apply, select an object, and just click your graphic style. If you wish to apply the graphic style and also keep the current settings make sure that you're holding down the ALT/OPTION key as you click the graphic style. Now that we covered the basics let's focus on the rest of these buttons and see how you can use them. As with the Appearance panel, all of these commands can also be accessed via the flyout menu from the Graphics Styles panel. First, of all, you should know that the "New Graphic Style" button can also be used to duplicate a graphic style. You'll learn in a few moments why you might want to duplicate one.

This "Break Link" button goes hand in hand with the "Redefine Graphic Style" command which can be found in the flyout menu of the Appearance panel. Let's say that you apply the same graphics style for several objects from your design, select just one of these objects, focus on the Appearance panel and as you can see Illustrator lets you know that you have a graphics style applied but clicking this "Break Link" button will cut the ties between the current Appearance settings and your saved graphics style so just click this button and the graphic style will disappear from the Appearance panel.

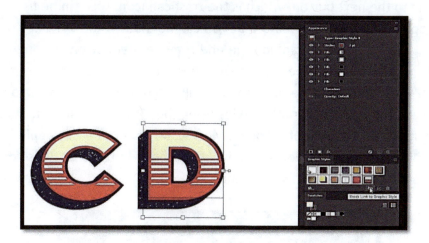

You can select another set of objects, make a quick adjustment, and now if you go to redefine graphic style your graphic style will be updated in the panel and all the instances where your graphics style is used will get updated as well. The only object that doesn't change its appearance is the one that you are linked to.

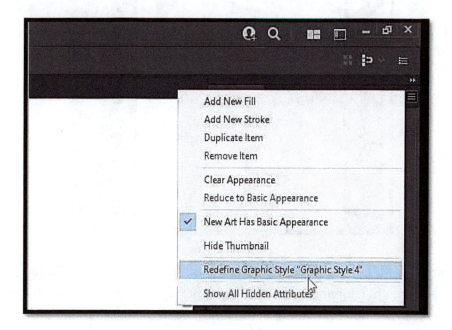

Now in some cases, you might want to keep both the original graphics style and the updated one - this is where the Duplicate graphic style command can come in handy. Drag the graphic style on top of the "New Graphic Style" button to easily duplicate it. You can then make the color changes and go again to redefine graphic style to update your graphic style. Moving to the next button, which is the trashcan icon; this can be used to remove selected graphic styles. Keep in mind that you can hold down the CTRL key or the SHIFT key to select more than one graphic style and remove them at once using this button. Once saved, graphic styles can be easily shared between Illustrator documents. Using the flyout menu you can open some panels with built-in graphic styles which you can easily apply, you can save your own graphic styles using the "Save Graphic Style" command or you can open some other sets of graphic styles. Again, you can easily apply any of these graphic styles, and now that you know what all these buttons do let's focus on the remaining commands from this flyout menu.

Starting with the Merge graphic styles command, let's say that you have two graphic styles that you wish to combine into a single graphic style, all you have to do is hold down the CTRL key to select both of these graphic styles, open the flyout menu and go to Merge graphic styles. Give this new graphic style a name; click OK to add it inside the Graphics Styles panel and now you can easily apply it. Next, you have the "Select all unused" command. This feature can be pretty useful whenever you wish to quickly clean up the Graphics Styles panel as it selects all of the unused graphic styles which you can then delete using the Delete button. Select "sort by name" from this drop-down menu whenever you wish to reorganize your graphics styles based on their names.

You can easily rename a graphic style as long as you have it selected. Just go to Graphics Styles options, type in your new name, and remember to click OK or press ENTER to apply the changes. You can check one of these two options (Live Square for Preview or Use Text for Preview) to preview your graphic styles either applied on text or a shape and besides this default thumbnail view, you have another two view options which can be pretty useful if you wish to always see the name of your graphic style using one of these List view modes. Keep in mind that you can right-click on any of your Graphics Styles for a larger preview. Finally, the "Override Character Color" feature will only affect the text from your design. Keep it enabled if you wish to remove the current text color as you apply a graphic style and if you disable this feature the graphic style will be applied to your text without removing the text color.

CC Libraries

One of the best things about Creative Cloud is the CC Libraries panel. It is extremely useful in all CC applications but in this section, we will take a close look at its role in Adobe Illustrator. Since the introduction of Creative Cloud libraries, Photoshop, Illustrator, InDesign, and other Adobe applications have become better connected than ever before. In this section, we are going to give you a brief introduction about how it works and if you are a Creative Cloud subscriber this is something you must try out yourself.

How it works

The panel that you need is under the Window menu and it's called Libraries. Open that up and you can create as many libraries as you want; normally it would be a library either for a project or a client or even a type of work that you do and these libraries would be accessible from all the other Adobe applications as well.

How to save an asset into a Creative Cloud library

If you select any of your illustrations, all you have to do is simply drag and drop it and when you let go it will be added as a graphic after which you can easily rename it. You can select another one and again drag and drop it in and now it's saved.

If you select a text object it is best to decide how you want to import this by choosing "Add content" and checking the attribute that you wish to save so it can be saved as a graphic style or just simply the color that you used on it.

Let's try that. First, turn off the rest and choose "Add." As you can see, it will show up as a color but then if you choose the graphic option it will be saved as an outline artwork. Once again, if you go back and choose Character style this time then it will be saved as a style which means that you can easily apply it to any text that you have in Adobe applications which includes not only Illustrator but also InDesign and Photoshop.

Working with the Library

Just to show you how quickly you can reuse any of these elements, switch to an empty document then bring one of your graphics by dragging and dropping it. You can scale it since it's completely vector-based but you might notice that it says it's a linked file and that is because it is connected to your Creative Cloud library. This means you can edit this by choosing Edit Original but then that also means it will be updated on all your projects wherever it was used since you added this to your Creative Cloud library.

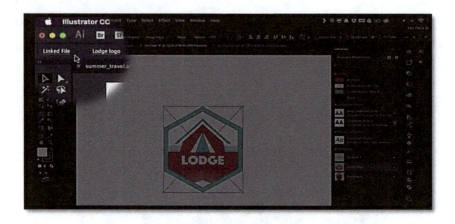

If you change the wording here then save this and go up to File > Save, this will update in the library as well and if you come back to your actual empty project it shows up there but not only there this time, it will also update in the other document. Using Creative Cloud library assets is very similar to working with symbols but they are even more advanced than symbols because they can be used in different Adobe applications at the same time and they will update in all of them at once when you edit and make a change on the original asset. Another thing you can use the Libraries panel for is to search on the Adobe stock website. Let's say you're looking for a tent, you're just going to type that here and this is going to search for images but you can look for illustration specifically or you can even choose vectors as the filtering option.

The cool thing is that if you find something that you like, you can add this to your library. You can save this and it will show up as a graphic here and you can even drag and drop it into your project. The issue here is that because it's not a licensed asset it's going to have a watermark on it but then it's still good to preview and check whether it's going to work with the style that you're working on and if your creative director or the client approves it then you can buy the license for it which would be as simple as right-clicking on it and choosing "License image."

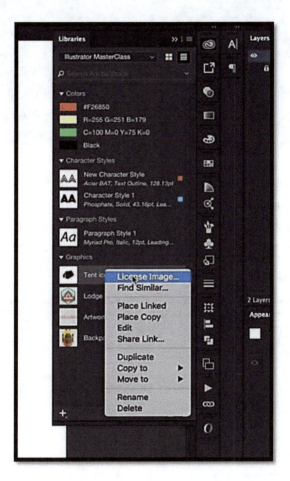

Share and collaborate

If you want to build up a library that you would like to make public and make it accessible to other Creative Cloud users you can do that from the panel menu by choosing "Share link."

Once you click on this it will open up a browser window where you can turn the private option on to public which will immediately generate a link you can also decide whether you want to allow people to follow which means that they can see but not download your assets. If you allow "save as" then that means they can save copies of your assets into their own projects.

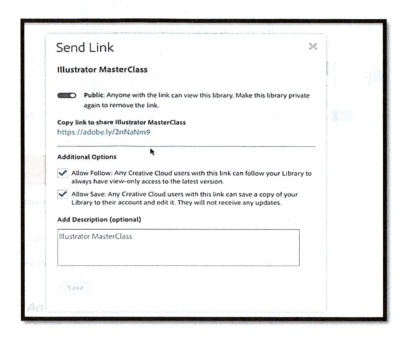

Similar to sharing your library you can invite creative who are also Creative Cloud subscribers to collaborate and add their own assets into the same Creative Cloud library. The way you do that from the browser is by clicking on the plus sign which will invite the collaborators. You just have to add their email address and decide whether they can edit or just view the library and while you are in the browser and going through your account you can also check all the libraries that you created, make changes to them, or even delete them. That's only something you can do from the browser.

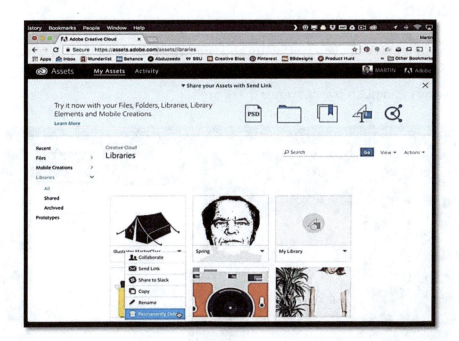

You can also find your mobile creations here which will display the different things that you've done in the Adobe mobile apps so if you haven't started using Creative Cloud libraries yet we highly recommend giving them a go because they can really streamline your creative workflow.

Review Questions

1. How can professional graphic designers use graphic styles in Adobe Illustrator to make their designs even better?
2. Give 5 tips for working faster and better with Adobe Illustrator as a professional graphic designer.
3. How do you save your assets in Adobe CC?

CHAPTER 15

DESIGN A T-SHIRT TEMPLATE

In this chapter, we are going to show you a quick way to design a T-shirt template using Adobe Illustrator.

Get started

A 14 X 18 document is what you start with, and then you insert your photo. What we need to do is cut out the background and a way that we do this is to take the Pen tool then go around the shirt and put a transparency mask on it.

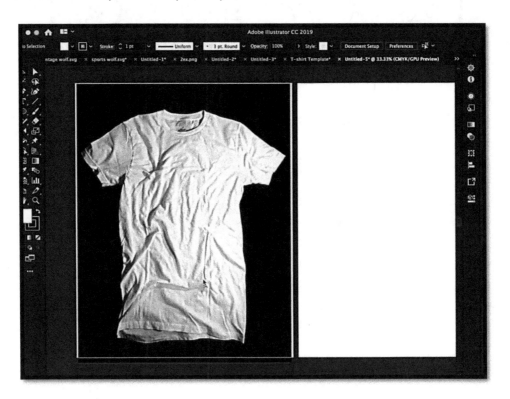

Applying strokes and fill

Now that we've got this shape we just need to go ahead and flip the strokes to fill and go into our Layers panel. We are going to copy that layer and then lock that layer down. This layer is very important.

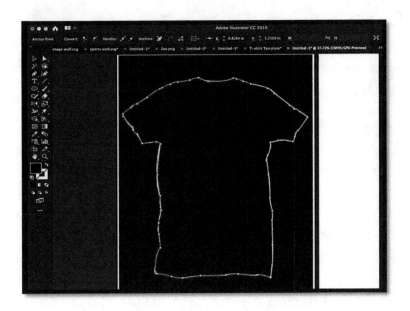

Applying transparency

Now we will go into our Shirt file and hit the transparency icon right here. If you don't see that you have to go into Window, down to Transparency, and click that. It will create that transparency icon for you. Also, make sure that you turn off the icons for the path that you just made.

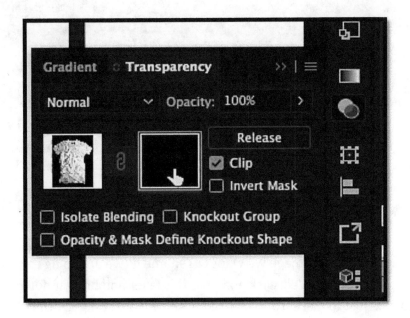

In this transparency, we want to go ahead and make a mask that should take everything out of the game. If we click on that mask or that black spot and we hit CTRL/COMMAND+F we'll paste in that shape that we just created. If we invert the mask we'll get the t-shirt cut out of the background.

Going deeper using the layers panel

We've just told you how to cut things out of the background in Illustrator. Now if we click back on this picture it'll bring back our Layers panel. A lot of times, people want to make sure that this is cut so they don't want to worry about the transparency and that's not a bad idea if you're like that what you want to do is to go to an object and rasterize and in this Rasterize icon make sure that you hit "transparent" for the background and hit OK. Doing that gets rid of the transparency mask and if used to move the t-shirt outside of the box you will see that the background is gone permanently.

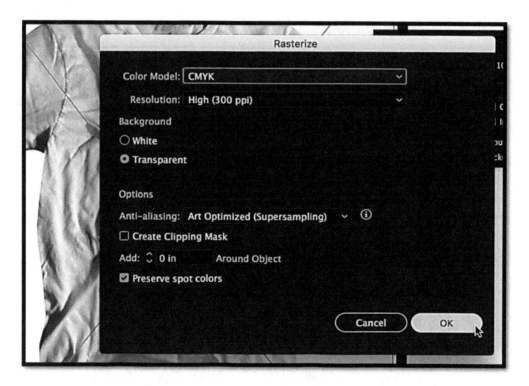

Now we're going to take the image we want to rename it (we are going to name it T-shirt) and then make a copy of it. We'll click and hold this layer and bring it down to the "New" icon at the bottom just to make a duplicate copy and we are going to bring this copy above the path that we created. Now of course we don't have clipping masks which means that anything that we make will affect everything under it but because this t-shirt is cut up to a shape nothing behind this will be disturbed if we put something behind it.

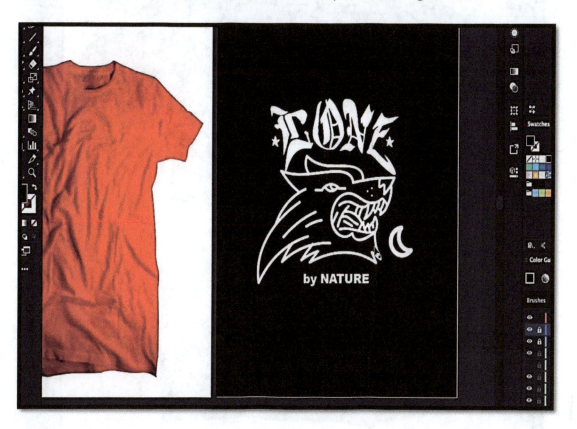

What we are saying is when we put this t-shirt on a multiply effect layer in the transparencies, of course, the t-shirt gets darker because it's affecting the actual t-shirt layer. We don't have this icon here but if we were to unlike the path and turn on this icon is only affecting the black layer so if we change the color of this black layer to red, we have just changed the color of the shirt and this looks pretty good. What we are going to do is name this layer and lock that layer down for a second. Now we want to go into Layer Two and we're going to use the other side of the artboard to start doing some art. What we want to do is to paste in some art quickly and then put a black background behind it as well so we can see what's going on.

We can also change the color of the shirt to black as well so we are just going to copy this layer quickly, go ahead and lock that down then go into our t-shirt template and just make a new layer above that. We can just go ahead and hit CTRL/COMMAND+F and paste that in. Now we have our t-shirt template.

Review Questions

1. Explain how you can make a t-shirt template using Adobe Illustrator.
2. Explain the use of the Layers panel in organizing your work.
3. How can you add your graphics to a template in Adobe Illustrator?

CHAPTER 16
WORKING WITH IMAGES

In this chapter, we'll be sharing with you how to import an image to Adobe Illustrator. If this is your first time using Adobe Illustrator and you don't know how to go about importing images and locking an image so that if you're working on that image it won't be moving around on the canvas, this chapter is dedicated to showing you basic steps on how to import your own image.

How to insert image in Adobe Illustrator

Adobe Illustrator is not like any other software that has an Import option as some basic software do. In Adobe Illustrator what we have is "Place." so we can use "Place" as our Import function. As you can see we have Export and under that, we have Export, Export to Screen, and Export As.

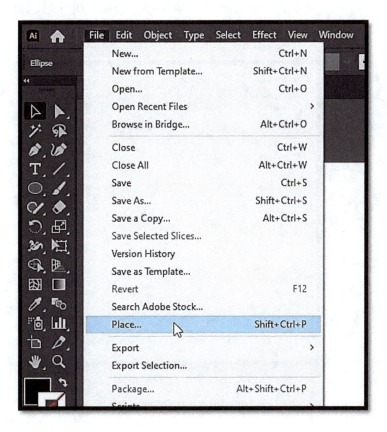

To import an image to Adobe Illustrator for the first time, head to the File menu at the top then scroll down and click on "Place." The shortcut for place is SHIFT+CTRL+P. Now if you click on that, it will take you to your folder where you have the list of all the work you have. There are different ways in which you can import an image to Adobe Illustrator. You can import it as a template link if you want to use it to replace the existing one and if you want to show Imports options so in the case of this chapter, we'll be sharing with you the easiest way. Click on the image you want to use, then click on "Place" and you'll see your image. Now it is left for you to place it on your workplace by clicking once and dropping it there. If you want to increase the size, rotate your image, or make it uniform, use ALT+SHIFT then you now increase or reduce it so that the shape will not deform because if you click on it now you might discover that it will deform. Also, if you want to place an image on your canvas make sure that it is centralized. If you move it closely you would realize that you see a center line there so ensure it is centered in your X and Y axis.

Embedding Images

This section will show you how to embed all images in Illustrator. First, go to the Window menu, go to Links, hold down the SHIFT key, and select the images from the dialogue box.

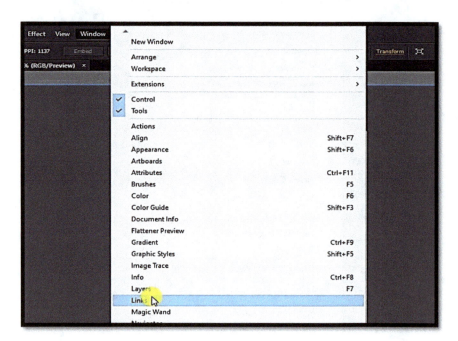

Then click on the menu icon at the top right corner and click on "Embed image."

Inserting an Image into a Shape

In this section, we'll be showing you how to insert an image into a shape in Adobe Illustrator. The first thing you want to do is to create the shape that you want to insert an image of so go over to the toolbar on the left side of your screen, Select the Shape Tool, and choose a shape. You can get these different shapes by right-clicking on the Shape icon right here and this displays all of the different options. For this illustration, select the Ellipse Tool then hold down SHIFT and ALT to create a circle. You can scale this up and give this color.

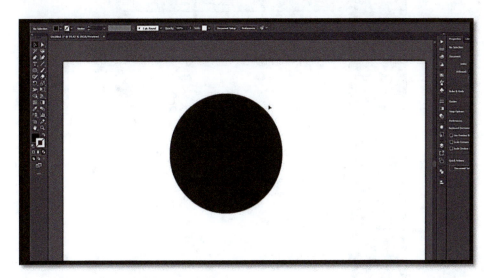

Now you're ready to insert the image into the shape. Press on the shape and on the Toolbar goes down to the icon that says "Draw inside." The keyboard shortcut for that is SHIFT+D.

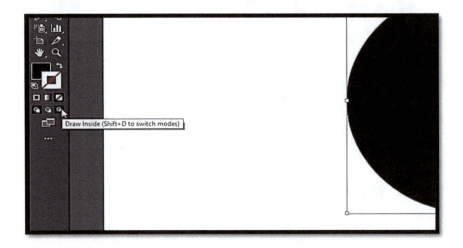

A border will appear around the circle and that's just fine. Now you want to press on the circle again then go up to File, down to Place (the keyboard shortcut for this is SHIFT+CTRL+P, then find the image that you have saved that you want to place into this shape so just select the image and press "Place."

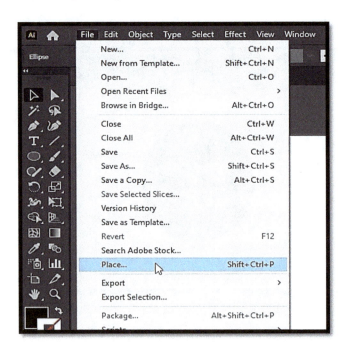

From here you want to drag around the shape and place it somewhere. When you have placed your image in this shape you can now just double-click on the artboard and you have now inserted an image in a shape.

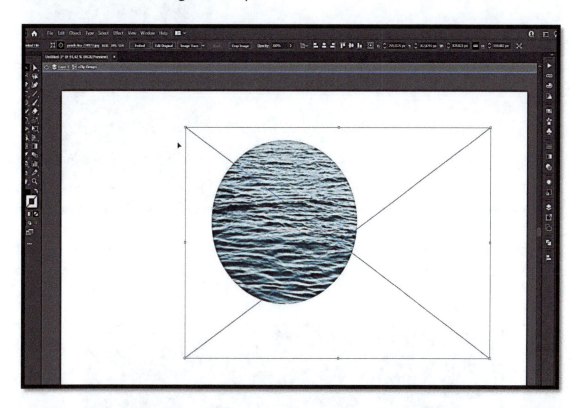

If you would like to change the image in this shape you can also double-click and change the position of this shape. This works with any shape you would like to use. You can also create shapes with the Pen Tool and this will still work.

Embedding Linked Images

In this section, we're going to show you how to embed a linked image here in Illustrator. Get your image then go ahead and place it on your Artboard as a linked image. With that image selected, go to the Properties panel, (if you don't see it it's going to be in the Window menu), at the very top you can see it is a linked file (it says that right here). Now if you click on this linked file you'll also see a little link icon indicator.

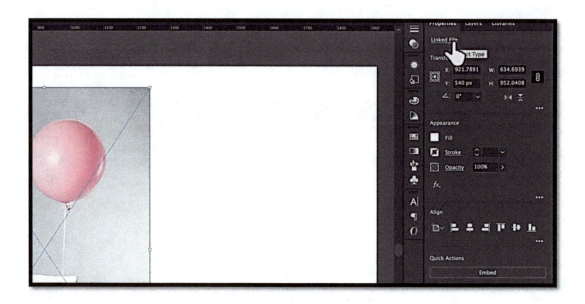

You can use this drop-down arrow right here to show more information about the link like the location of the file as well as the resolution and dimensions and some other details.

If you want to embed this image you would go up here to the hamburger menu drop-down from there. You'd see an embed image option.

One important note here is: that this linked file needs to exist on your computer or your storage so it can't be a missing link or else it can't embed the image, however, if you have this image linked properly you can click this embed image option and it will remove the link property of that image and will embed it into your file. One other thing to note here is your file will increase by the size of that image because the image is now contained within the file so in this case, 1.6 megabytes is about how much bigger this illustrator file will be when you save it down. This matters a lot when you start to embed a lot of imagery into your Illustrator documents.

Review Questions

1. How can you add images to Adobe Illustrator to make your artwork better?
2. Explain how to make images bigger or smaller in Adobe Illustrator without losing quality.
3. What tools in Adobe Illustrator can you use to edit and improve your images?

CHAPTER 17

MASKING IN ADOBE ILLUSTRATOR

In this chapter, we're going to talk about a bunch of different types of masks here in Adobe Illustrator.

Clipping Mask

With this, you can simply use a shape to instantly contain your artwork within a specific area. This means you create the shape that you want to put your artwork within and that shape is going to be the mask.

How to Create Clipping Mask

Get started by creating a new canvas. You can create any size you want by changing the height and the width in the document window then go to the Tools panel and select the Ellipse Tool. Move to the top and choose a fill or color, hold ALT and SHIFT to draw a perfect shape then center the shape onto the canvas by clicking on the Alignment icons. Next, import the photo by going to File > Place, choose the photo and press ENTER. Click on the canvas to release the photo, hold down the SHIFT and ALT keys at the same time, and resize it from one anchor point. Drag and place it onto the shape, hold ALT and SHIFT to resize the photo proportionally, right-click on the photo, and send it behind the shape. Press CTRL+A to select all. You can also drag over it to do the same. Go to Object> Clipping Mask > Make. Better still, you can use the shortcut CTRL+7 to do the same.

Now let's say you want to adjust the photo to your preference and drag it but realize it moves along with the shape and you wouldn't want that to happen, press Ctrl+Z to undo the action then go to Object > Clipping Mask > Edit content. Select the photo and position it how you want, hold ALT and SHIFT to resize the photo proportionally. You can see it cutting out the shape while resizing the photo.

Go to the Layers panel and open the group accordingly. Select the photo right-click on it and choose "Isolated Clipping Mask." Hold Alt and SHIFT again and then resize the photo. Finally, click on the arrow to close the Layers panel.

Editing your Clipping Mask

When you select your Clipping Mask you'll see up in the upper-left corner of the Illustrator window an icon called the Clip Group and it has two buttons next to it allowing you to either edit the clipping path or the contents.

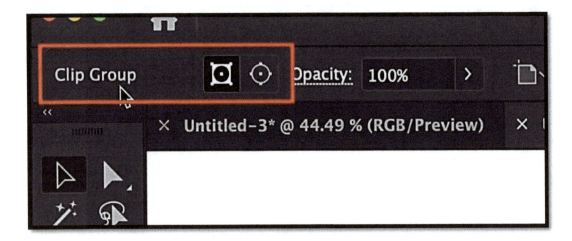

When you click on the Contents button with that image selected, you can reposition it inside of the clipping mask. You need a way of getting at the individual parts of this clip group because if you just select the whole clip group like any other group in Illustrator, these bounding box edits apply to everything so you can wind up accidentally squeezing your photograph. To edit a clipping mask you can either use the buttons on the top control bar or you can treat this like any other group in Illustrator and switch back and forth between your Selection Tool and your Direct Selection Tool. For example, you can deselect the "Clip Group" and then grab your white arrow by tapping A on your keyboard then you can select the photograph inside, and move it around inside of the clipping shape.

Now if you want to select the shape you can click on its edge with your white arrow and then switch to your black arrow and now you can edit the shape without disturbing the photograph so whether you use the buttons on the top control bar or you use your Selection Tools, either way, you can decide which part of the clipping mask you want to edit. It's also helpful to look at clip groups in the Layers panel. Here in the Layers panel, we have layer 1. If we go ahead and expand this layer, we can see the clip group. If we expand that again, inside that we have the rectangle; that's our clipping path and the linked file is our image.

213

We can just deselect here by clicking on the artboard and then go in and individually select either the image or the rectangle so here's yet another way to select the individual components of this clip group. Also, while we have this shape selected it has an underline underneath it so this is how we know that this is the clipping path. Now that we have it selected we can certainly do more edits as we did before but we also want to point out that over here at the bottom of the Tool panel, we have no fill and no stroke so that's something that happens when you create a path or shape and use it as a mask; once you do that, that shape becomes invisible with no fill and no stroke appearance and that remains the same even if we release this clipping mask. If we go with the clipping mask selected up to the Object menu right back to where we have Clipping Mask and then choose "Release," now we no longer have our Clip Group. If we look over in layer one we just have a rectangle with no fill and no stroke on top of our linked file.

That's how to make a Clipping Mask in Illustrator and knowing it from this perspective is going to help you when you get into more complex clip groups where you have lots of objects and nested groups.

Opacity Masks

In this section, we are going to explain what Opacity Masks are in Adobe Illustrator by showing you a couple of quick examples of how they can be applied to your illustrations. An opacity mask is something that you can apply to any object that you create giving you the ability to define the transparency of the object with more control. This will help you add visibility to your designs in creative and dynamic ways. For this illustration, we have created a simple vector bird that we want to make a bit more exciting by adding textures and gradients and we are going to do this by using Opacity Masks. You can follow along using any illustration you have created in Adobe Illustrator.

Before we begin, ensure you have opened the Transparency and Gradient panels which can be found under the Windows menu. The Transparency panel is where the Opacity Masks live. To show you how this works we are going to start by creating a shadow on the bird, select the bird's peach-colored body, copy and paste in place then go to our fuel box and choose a slightly darker color to the pink. With your object selected, you should be able to see a thumbnail image to the left of your Transparency panel.

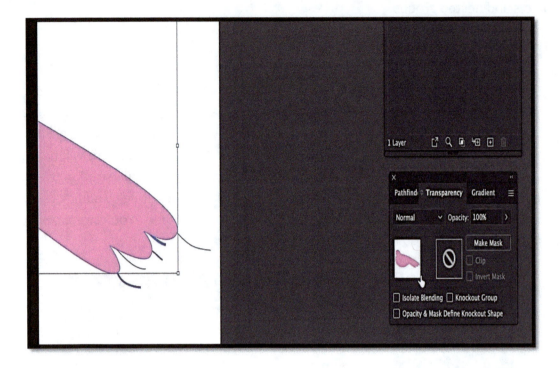

To create an Opacity Mask for this object double-click inside the empty box to the right, you will notice that your object has disappeared and the box is now black; this is Adobe Illustrator's default and it means that your object will have an opacity of 0%. In the Opacity Mask the transparency values are represented as different shades of gray. Anything black in your Opacity Mask has an opacity of 0% and is invisible, while anything white in your Opacity Mask has an opacity of hundred percent and is visible. Any areas with different shades of gray will vary in transparency depending on their color.

We're going to apply a grayscale gradient to this Opacity Mask. To do this, you need to go to the Gradient panel in the drop-down menu, select a grayscale gradient, and then you need to create a vector object in the Opacity Mask. In this instance, we're going to create a rectangle that covers the entire bird's body and we can see our pink object now fades out as its transparency values are determined by the grayscale gradient. We have just added to the Opacity Mask so if we go to the Opacity Mask thumbnail in our Transparency panel you can now see that it contains the gradient we have just added.

Let's try another way of using Opacity Mask. To go back to editing your illustration you need to exit the Opacity Mask by clicking once on the left thumbnail of the object then with this object selected, we'll go to our Layers panel and just move it behind a few different objects so the eyes and the features on the bird can stand out.

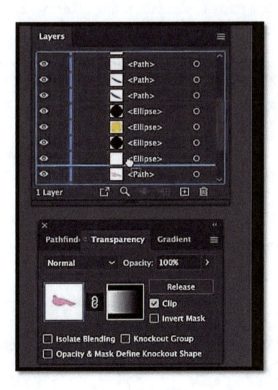

The next opacity mask we want to add is to the squiggly lines on the bird's tail. We want these lines to be contained to the bird's tail and not hanging out the ends. First, we are going to select all the lines and ensure that they are grouped as one object by right-clicking and selecting "Group." In the Transparency panel we can now see the lines represented as one object in the thumbnail.

We'll go back to our illustration and select the bird's body, copy and paste in place, and then in the Field box, we'll choose white. We'll copy the white object, and then delete it from our artboard, select the squiggly lines again, and create an Opacity Mask by double-clicking on the right box in the Transparency panel. Again, everything is defaulted to black and nothing is visible. We'll paste in place the white object we saved previously and now the lines are contained within the tail.

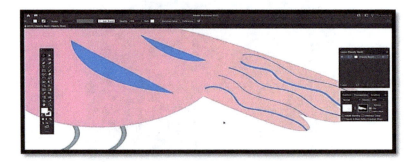

Review Questions

1. Why do we use masks in Adobe Illustrator?
2. Explain how to create a mask in Adobe Illustrator and use it to show or hide parts of our artwork.
3. What are some cool tricks you can do with masks in Adobe Illustrator, and how can you make them even more interesting by combining them with other tools?

CHAPTER 18
SAVING AND SHARING YOUR CREATIONS

Being able to share what you create with others is one of the reasons why we create. From sharing your art on social media with friends to sharing professional designs with coworkers, sharing your work for fun or collaboration has become more important than ever. Illustrator gives you lots of options for both saving and sharing your work in different formats for different purposes. We know you want to jump in and try this yourself, but let's first check out some examples of what we're talking about. Now, let's say you're making a graphic for social media, you set up your project and you start working. Unless you finish your project in one go, you're probably going to need to save your file so you can keep working later (we've all lost work because we forgot to hit Save). So Illustrator gives you a couple of different ways to make life easier.

Saving for the first time?

When you save for the first time by choosing "File," "Save" or you save a copy of a document, you can either save your work to your hard drive as an Illustrator file or online as a Cloud document. Whichever way you save, this will be your working dock where everything is preserved.

If you share it with someone, they can make edits too in Illustrator. When you save to your hard drive, it's like any file you save to your computer. You can attach it to an email or upload it to your preferred file-sharing service. But it only exists on your hard drive. So you'll need to create a backup manually.

Save to cloud

If you save your project as a Cloud document, it lives safely in Creative Cloud and is accessible from anywhere you log in. As a Cloud document, you can invite others to work on the file on their own computers by sharing the file. Cloud docs automatically save your work for you. You can even see a version history in the Version History panel and roll back to earlier drafts if you need to.

Share for review

Once you're done with your project, you might want to share it with others for review, probably to get final approval. You can save your project as a PDF by choosing "File," "Save as." Anyone can view the PDF even if they don't have Illustrator. They can use a free reader. Once approved, you're most likely to post the project on social media or website or anywhere else you need to post to a website or social media. You can either save the entire project or maybe just one part by choosing File, Export selection. You can save as a JPEG, a PNG, or another format and upload them where you need them. To recap, you can save your file in Creative Cloud or locally, whatever is best for your situation. When you're ready to share your project or part of your project, you can do so in a format that makes sense like a JPEG or a PNG for social media or a PDF for printing or review.

Save Illustrator file as JPEG

A JPEG image does not include transparency just so you know; you're going to have a white background if you have any sort of transparency in your document. If you want to save your Illustrator file as a JPEG you can go up to the File menu, down to Export and you can do "Export for screens" or "Export as."

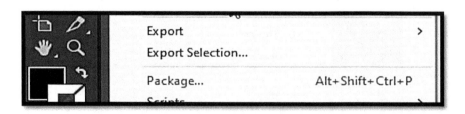

Export for screens gives you two tabs: your artboards or your assets. In the Asset Export panel you can take objects in your design, right-click them, and add them here and you can export them individually.

In the Artboards section, you're going to see all the artboards in your design and you can export them all at once or individually. On the right-hand side, you can see your selection of artboards. You can include the bleed or you can also export the full document (this means everything on and off your artboards) so if you choose this, it's going to export a JPEG of everything inside your Illustrator document.

You can then select where they save, whether you open it after export, you can create subfolders with different scales and formats and then you can select your formats down here. With this scaler here you can choose if you want 1x, like the size that it is in your document, or more. You can add a suffix and you can also change the file format. You can see other formats here but then JPEG 100 would be the best quality JPEG that you can export. You can add a prefix and then simply export your artboard. If you're creating thumbnails for something like a YouTube channel here in Illustrator you can export them as JPEG. To do that, go up to File down to Export and instead of Export for screens, choose "Export as." The "Export as" feature almost pulls up like the "Save" dialog box. Here, you can adjust the name but then when you want to select the format it might start on PNG so all you have to do is go down to JPEG. If you want to use Artboards you have to click "use artboards" or else this will export the full document like we showed before so click "use artboards," then select your artboard or a range of artboards or all and hit Export.

After you hit Export it's going to pull up some JPEG options. It's going to let you do different modes whether it's RGB or CMYK. You could even do grayscale, and select the quality (you can keep yours on 9 because thumbnails on YouTube are only two megabytes and 10 would give you a larger file than 2 megabytes) but you would use the maximum if you're trying to save the highest quality jpeg.

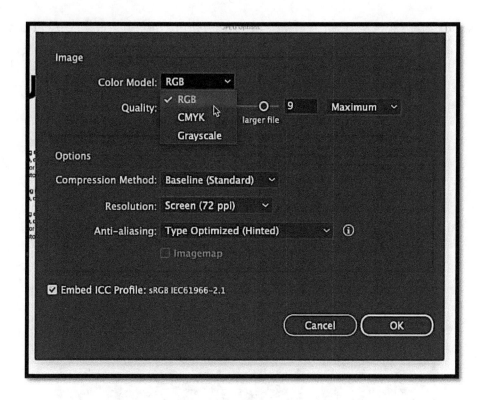

There are some compression modes here and the resolution, which is like the scale. If you have a 1920 x 1080 artboard and you export it at 72 pixels per inch that's going to export as 1920 x 1080. If you increase this, it's going to just double the size and almost triple the size on high or maybe even more. You can choose whether to export larger jpegs here and that's just going to increase the pixel count in the image. Now, remember, jpegs are raster files so they are going to be pixel-based, they will no longer be Vector but this is the way that you can export jpegs every day here in Illustrator.

Export Artboards as separate files

Let's say you have a project with four artboards and you want to export one artboard as a separate file, on the left side click on the Artboard Tool, click on the artboard and you can see the name of the artboard in the left corner. If you want to make some adjustments click on the artwork options in the Properties panel, click on Window, and check the Properties panel and you can change the name and size of the artboard. To save an artwork, go to File and "Save As" or "Save a copy." Let's say you want to save the second artboard, select a folder where you want to save it and click on Save. Now in this window, check the box that says "Save each artboard to a separate file." If you do this, all artboards will save it as a separate file and you will have four illustrator files.

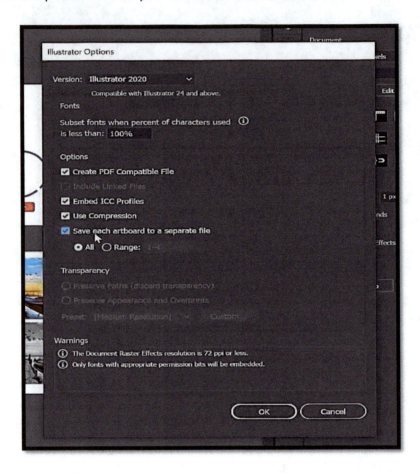

If you want to save just the second artboard click on the option that says "Range" and place 3 because you want to save the second artboard, then click on OK. Next, open the folder where you saved the second artboard and you can just rename it if you want and you have just the second artboard as a separate file.

Export with Transparency

Let's go over how you can export a graphic with a transparent background using Adobe Illustrator. To do that, make sure you have the object selected then right-click on it and go down to where it says "Export selection from" and the menu will pop up. In this menu, you'll see up here where it says Asset, go ahead and change the name of this to whatever you'd like your file name to be, and press ENTER.

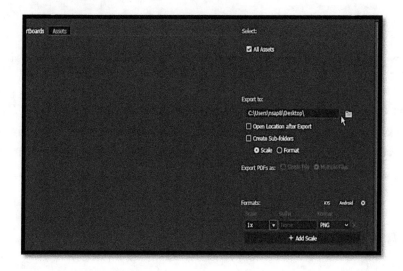

If you come over here to where it says "Export to" you can click on the folder menu to choose where on your hard drive you'd like to save the file and then down here you can choose your file types. Here you only have one file type chosen but if you have other file types listed here just go ahead and click the X next to them to get rid of them since all you need is one copy and you need it to be in PNG format because PNG is the format that supports transparent backgrounds so make sure you have that enabled. Make sure you have the suffix set to none (if there's anything in there just erase it) and then over here where it says Scale, make sure you have this set to 1x. If you have this set to anything more than 1x it's going to export it at a different size than what it currently is and once you've done that you can go ahead and click on the "Export Asset" button and now your graphic should be exported as a graphic with the transparent background. If you open up your exported PNG graphic with Photoshop, for instance, and zoom in on this graphic you can see that this is indeed a transparent graphic as indicated by the checkerboard background going around the edges.

Review Questions

1. How would you save your work in different file formats in Adobe Illustrator, and what factors should you consider when choosing the right format?
2. Explain how to export your Illustrator artwork for printing and what are some tips to make sure the colors and files look good.
3. How can you share your Illustrator creations with others, and what should you be careful about to protect your work?

CHAPTER 19
ILLUSTRATOR SHORTCUTS YOU MUST KNOW

Illustrator has an overwhelming amount of shortcuts, 233 to be exact. Thankfully you don't need to know all of them, but some are just essential, and in the long run, they can save you hours of work. So we have selected some that will help you. In this chapter, we'll explain to you why they're so important and also show you a few tricks about how to use them.

Group/Ungroup

Groups are one of the most useful features of Illustrator, and while you might think they're just there to organize content, they can be used to create specific visual effects. Some effects and properties in Illustrator are applied differently to groups than to single objects. Strokes can be moved behind the contents of a group in the Appearance Panel, creating a single outline for the whole group, instead of one outline for every object. Similarly, effects like Drop Shadow, Outer Glow, and Inner Glow also apply differently to groups, affecting the entire group as a whole. Transparency will also be applied to the group as a whole, instead of every single object within it. But perhaps the single reason we use groups the most is to align objects to the artboard. Let's say we have some objects and we want them to be on the center of the artboard. If we try to align them when they are ungrouped, they will just get stacked on top of each other, but if we group them before aligning, the align function will treat the group as a single object, perfectly placing the whole group in the center of the artboard, while not moving the objects within. Then, we can just ungroup them if needed.

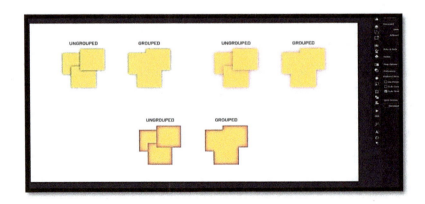

The shortcut for grouping objects is CTRL+G for Windows users, and CMD+G for Mac. For ungrouping, CTRL+SHIFT+G for Windows and CMD+SHIFT+G for Mac. The alternative way to group and ungroup is to either use the Object menu or the right-click menu.

Align

Since we're talking about aligning objects, this is our next shortcut. Unfortunately, Illustrator doesn't have shortcuts for aligning. Thankfully though, the align commands are available through the Object menu, and this means we can assign custom shortcuts to them. And yes, you can align using the Control Bar or the Align Panel, but all the icons look so similar, it always takes a few seconds to find the one you need, and for days, these seconds can stack to hours. So, let's create new shortcuts. Go to the Edit menu and choose Keyboard Shortcuts there. In the Shortcuts window, change the displayed shortcuts from Tools to Menu Commands. Then, navigate to Object and Align. Now, you can add whatever combination of keys you want.

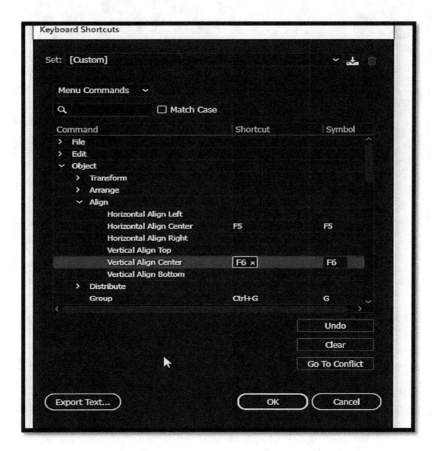

We like to use the F keys because they're usually bound to shortcuts in the Window menu, but we particularly never use them, so that's fine. You don't have to add shortcuts to every single alignment option, but at least add to Horizontal center and Vertical center. These are the ones you'll be using the most. And don't be afraid to override an existing shortcut if it's something you don't use, you can always restore Illustrator's default shortcuts later if you need to. When you're done, press OK and Illustrator will prompt you to save a shortcuts preset, so give it a name and then you're finished. Now, whenever you have objects selected, you can just press the shortcuts you assigned and the magic will happen. After a few days of using this, you won't be able to go back ever again. But if you want to restore Illustrator's default shortcuts, just open the Shortcuts window and choose "Illustrator Defaults" from the drop-down menu.

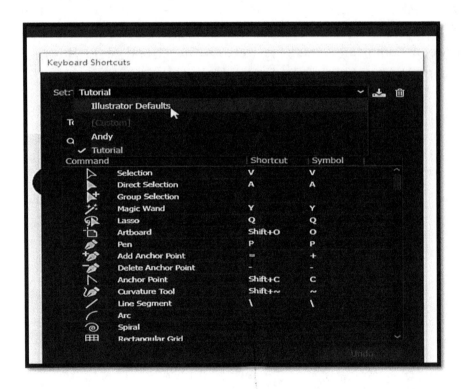

Clipping Masks

Moving on we have clipping masks, which are an essential feature in any design workflow. If you're unfamiliar with it, a clipping mask is a way to hide parts of the artwork using a specific shape, which can be anything from something as simple as a rectangle to custom, complex shapes. To create a clipping mask, you need to select all the objects you want to clip as well as the shape that will work as the mask itself, and Illustrator will always use the object that is on top of the stack as the mask. After you have everything selected, hit the shortcut CTRL+7 on Windows or CMD+7 on Mac to create the clipping mask and then you're done. If you want to release the clipping mask, you can use the shortcut CTRL+ALT+7 on Windows or CMD+OPTION+7 on Mac.

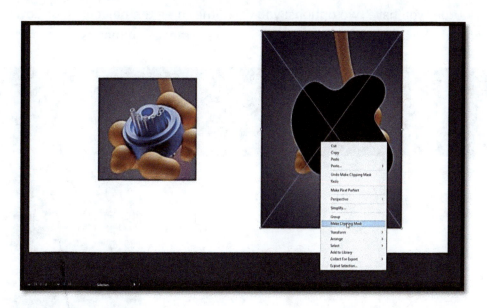

There is a cool trick to create clipping masks using text. First, outline the text by pressing CTRL+SHIFT+O, or CMD+SHIFT+O on Mac. Then, transform the text into a compound path using the shortcut CTRL+8 or CMD+8 on Mac. A compound path is needed when you want to create a clipping mask with more than one object. Then, just proceed with the clipping process as usual. The alternative way to make clipping masks is to use either the Object menu or the right-click menu.

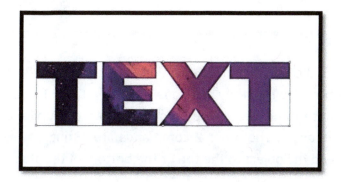

Arrange

To make it easier to change the stack order of your objects, it's essential to make good use of the Arrange commands. In Illustrator, objects are displayed following a stack order. If one object is above the other in the Layers Panel, so will it be on the Artboard. To change the stack order you have two options: you can either drag the objects up or down in the stack through the Layers Panel, or you can use the Arrange commands.

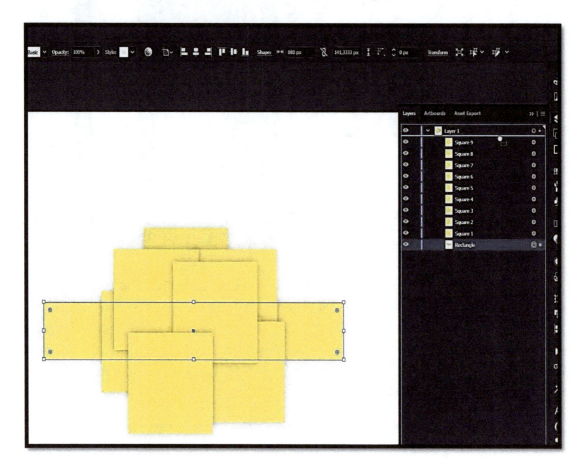

There are 4 of them: the first two are "Bring Forward" and "Send Backward." These will move the object up or down in the stack, one layer at a time. To do this, you can hold CTRL or CMD then use the close square bracket "]" to move up, and the open square bracket "[" to move down. The other 2 commands are "Bring to Front" and "Send to Back." These will send the object to the top or the bottom of the stack.

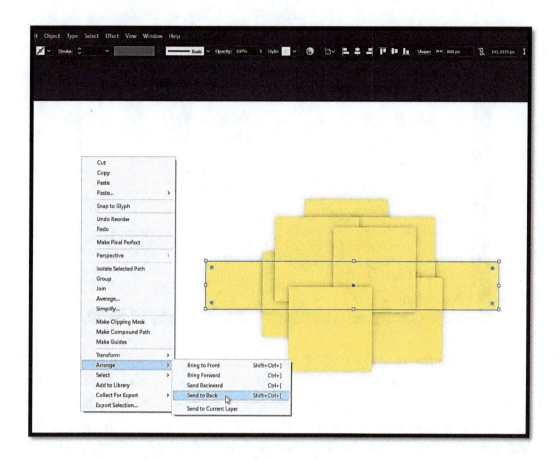

The shortcut is similar, but you must also hold SHIFT. So, CTRL or CMD+SHIFT+] (close square bracket) to bring the object to the top of the stack, and CTRL or CMD+SHIFT+[(open square bracket) to send the object to the bottom of the stack. The alternative way to access the Arrange commands is to use either the Object menu or the right-click menu.

Transform again

Sometimes working in Illustrator can get a little repetitive. Sometimes you have to create multiples of the same objects, or just duplicate something a bunch of times. We get it, it's boring. That's where the "Transform Again" command comes in handy. This little-known command does a pretty specific task: it repeats on the selected object the last transformation you made. This can be moving, rotating, scaling, or duplicating. Let's show you this in action. Let's say we want to move an object a few pixels to the side. If we now use the Transform Again command, shortcut CTRL, or CMD+D, we can see that the action is repeated, and every time we use the command it repeats it again and again, moving the same amount in the same direction. It even works if we select a different object.

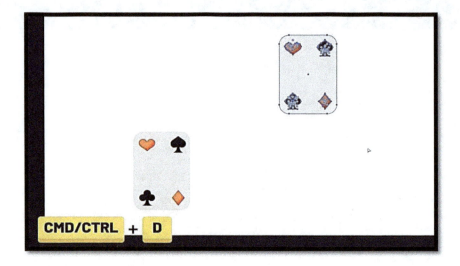

To make it more interesting, instead of just moving, we are going to hold the ALT or OPTION key while dragging the object. Holding ALT creates a duplicate of the object, and now if we use the Transform Again command, it repeats the entire action, creating a new duplicate every time, always in the same direction. Now we can select the entire row and repeat the process downwards. We drag the first time holding ALT and then press CTRL+D to repeat the action. Quite quickly, we've created a deck of cards. But what if we need to be more precise?

Let's try working with rotation. We are going to create a circle on the artboard using the Ellipse Tool, shortcut L, and then we are going to select the Rotate Tool, shortcut R, hold the ALT or OPTION key, and click once on top of the right anchor point of the circle. By holding ALT and clicking somewhere with the Rotate Tool, two things happen: we open the rotate window, so we can precisely input how much we want to rotate, but we also change the reference point of the rotation from the center of the object to the place where we clicked. Now, we can just input a rotation amount, let's say 20 degrees, and instead of clicking OK, we'll click on copy. This will create a new copy of the object, rotated 20 degrees around the reference point.

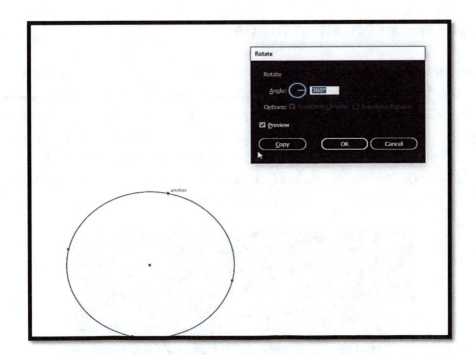

If we now select the copy and hit CTRL or CMD+D it will repeat this process of copy and rotation, and just like so we can easily create some very interesting shapes in Illustrator.

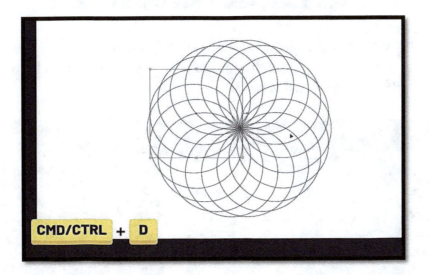

The possibilities of this command are endless, but it might take some getting used to. The alternative way to access the Transform Again command is either through the Object menu or the right-click menu.

Trim view/Presentation mode

Sometimes things can get a little messy in our file, so it's great to have a quick way to preview the things we're creating without all these elements getting in the way. Thankfully, a few versions ago, Illustrator introduced Trim View and Presentation Mode, two amazing features to preview your work. The bad news: both of them don't have shortcuts. The good news: you already know how to create them. They're located under the View menu. Our keys of choice are F11 for Trim View and F12 for Presentation Mode, but you can choose whatever you want. Let's see how each one works.

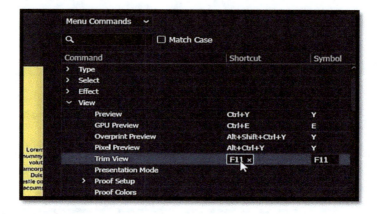

Trim View simply hides everything that is placed outside the artboard. Objects are still there, you can still select them, but they are hidden so you can have a better picture of how the artwork will look when it is exported.

Presentation Mode, on the other hand, actually turns Illustrator into a PowerPoint of some sort. It will make Illustrator go full screen, with the artboard taking up most of the space, and hiding the user interface. It also prevents you from selecting anything in the artboard. Clicking anywhere or using the arrow keys will skip to the next artboard. One way we like to use Presentation Mode is when we are too lazy to export a design and send it for review. We just press F12 to go to Presentation Mode, use Windows Capture Tool to take a Screenshot of the artboard, and then just paste it on Discord or any other messaging app.

Expand/Expand Appearance

Expanding a vector object in Illustrator is just as useful as it is confusing, especially since we have two similar commands: Expand and Expand appearance. Let's understand what each one does once and for all. Both commands can be accessed through the Object menu, and in a general sense they do the same thing: they convert appearance attributes, which are literally what the name implies, into objects.

You can see an object's attributes through the Appearance panel - each layer on the panel is a different attribute. When you expand a shape, the attributes, like strokes, gradients, effects, or a blend will be converted to separate objects. The only difference between the two commands is that expand is used when the object only has basic attributes, like fill, stroke, and opacity. The Expand appearance is used when the object has other attributes applied to it, such as an envelope distortion, a drop shadow, or a distortion effect.

For example, let's apply a Twist effect on a rectangle. We can still edit the original rectangle and the Twist effect will adjust accordingly. This happens because the effect is applied as an attribute in the Appearance panel, and so the original shape is preserved. If we want to convert this effect into an object, or, effectively, apply this distortion to the rectangle, we can use the Expand Appearance command.

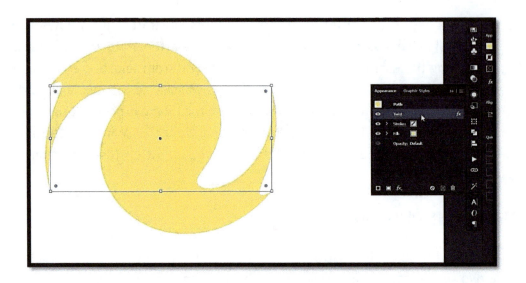

Now, the effect no longer shows up in the Appearance panel and we no longer have access to the original shape. It has been converted into its object, made out of paths and anchor points. We can do a similar thing with strokes. If you have an object that has a stroke, you can convert the stroke into a separate object by using the Expand command. Just select Stroke in the window that pops up and hit OK. Both of these commands don't have default shortcuts, so we have to create new ones again. Our shortcuts of choice for Expand and Expand appearance are CTRL+SHIFT+1 and CTRL+SHIFT+2, respectively. Replace CTRL for CMD if you're a Mac user, at this point we believe you got it already.

Review Questions

1. Why are shortcuts important in Adobe Illustrator?
2. List the shortcuts for arranging and grouping objects in Adobe Illustrator.
3. How can beginners remember and practice the most important shortcuts in Adobe Illustrator effectively?

CHAPTER 20

ILLUSTRATOR SECRETS GRAPHIC DESIGNERS MUST KNOW

In this chapter, you're going to learn 30 things in Adobe Illustrator that all graphic designers need to know and this bag of tricks will save you time, reduce frustration, and ultimately make your creative life so much easier.

Copy Appearance

To copy appearance effects from one object to another select both, go to the Layers panel, find the layer with the effects you'd like to copy, hold ALT or OPTION, and drag one circle onto the other and all of the appearance effects are now copied over.

Easily create dotted lines

Let's start by drawing a line, thicken up that stroke weight and if we open up the Stroke panel we can check the box of the dashed line, set the dash to zero and the gap to whatever you like. Change the Gap type to round and you now have a dotted line. You can change the distance by adjusting the Gap value.

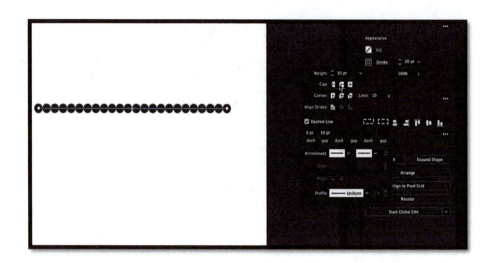

Intertwine two overlapping circles

If you have two overlapping circles select them go to object menu, down to Intertwine and select "Make," get rid of helpful but slightly annoying pop-up and then drag over an area where the shapes intersect to intertwine them both.

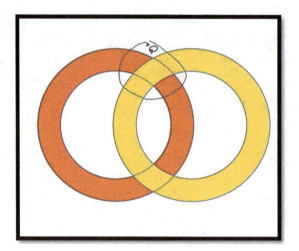

Get trimmed preview

If your artwork extends beyond the bounce of the artboard go to View and "**Trim view**" to get a trimmed preview.

Flip the direction of a curved line

If you select the Arc Tool and click and drag to draw a curved line, while drawing the Line you can press F to flip the direction.

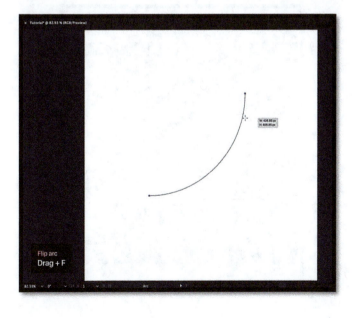

Clean up crooked curves

Select the Pencil Tool and then draw a squiggly line. As you can see this is pretty awful but if you go back to this menu and click and hold you can select the Smooth Tool and using this you can click and drag repeatedly to go over the line to smooth out all of these curves. This is a great way to clean up any janky curves.

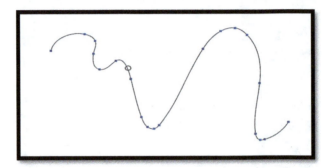

Switch to Smooth Tool

Following on from that double-click the Pencil Tool and then go and check the option here that says "Option key toggles to Smooth Tool." Now when you draw a squiggly line, you can hold down ALT or OPTION, which is a shortcut to switch to the Smooth Tool.

Cut straight line

We have a big red circle and want to cut this with the Knife Tool so with this tool selected we're going to click and drag, holding SHIFT and it doesn't cut a straight line. The solution is you need to hold down ALT or OPTION and SHIFT to cut straight lines. Once you've made some clean cuts you can now separate the shape into individual pieces.

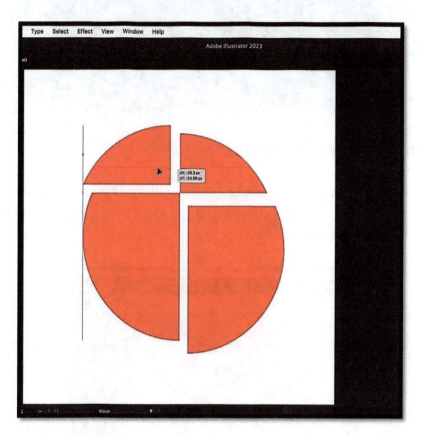

Highlight the end of a stroke

Let's say we have a gradient running from left to right. Let's select the shape and go to the Gradient panel, make sure the stroke is selected and we can now click through the options to change how the gradient is applied to a stroke. For example, if we select the middle one and then bring the right edge of the slider in we can now add a highlight to the very end of that stroke.

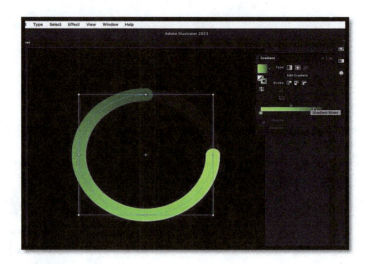

Reshape an existing shape

Did you know you can draw over an existing shape with the Pencil Tool and it will reshape it? Let's say we have a big pink circle, we'll just draw some eyes, change the color to white, duplicate them, and make them black.

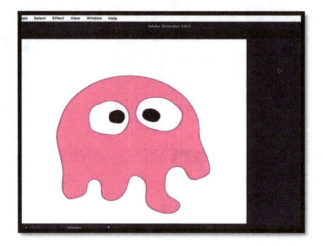

Get smoother curves

Here's another one with the Pencil Tool. Draw a terrible line and double-click the Pencil Tool. You can drag the slider to the right if you'd like smoother curves. Let's try that same curve again and you can see less accuracy but much smoother.

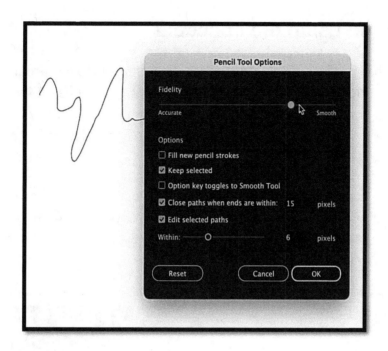

Use arrow keys to adjust a shape

Next, we're going to select the Star Tool, click and drag to draw a star, and then use the up and down arrow keys to adjust the number of points. You can also hold down COMMAND or CTRL and drag to adjust the size of the radius.

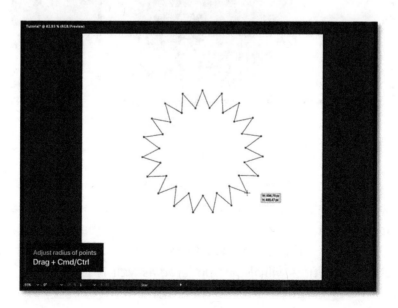

Move around using the spacebar

Did you know the spacebar is a shortcut to use the Hand Tool to pan around? You can use COMMAND or CTRL plus or minus to zoom in or out. You can press Z for the Zoom Tool and COMMAND or CTRL+0 fits the artboard to the screen.

Using global swatches

We've got some icons. If you go to the Swatch panel and scroll down you can double-click one of the global swatches. Make sure that the global option is checked and if you enable Preview and adjust the sliders, any change to a global Swatch will be updated throughout the entire document. This is very useful.

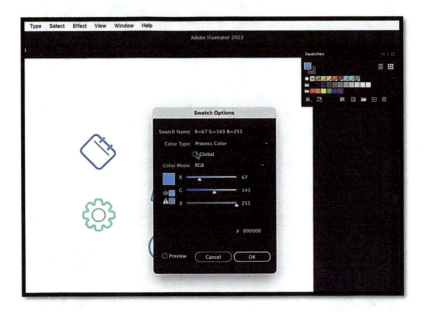

Applying tints

Now let's take a look at Tints. First, go to Window and down to Color. Select one of these icons with a global Swatch, switch over to Color guide, and make sure you set the base color. Now you can click through the Tints to apply a tint of that same global Swatch and the great thing about this is if you go and edit the original color of the global Swatch, let's say red, all of the related tints will also be updated as well.

Editing a new document

How do you edit a new document? You can go to Document Setup and change a few things but you can also select the Artboard Tool and change the artboard's width and height from the top right corner. To change the DPI you need to go to **Effect** and select Document Raster Effects Settings and from the drop-down you can change the Color mode or the DPI and you can also scroll to the bottom of the File menu if you'd like to switch between the CMYK and RGB color modes.

Rearrange Artboards

So we have an artboard with the Artboard Tool, let's add a few more artboards. If you encounter any issues, you can fix this mess by rearranging everything, choosing the layout type, you can adjust the number of columns, set the spacing between artboards and that's it.

Get a wireframe preview

- Go to View down to Outline to get a wireframe preview of your design.

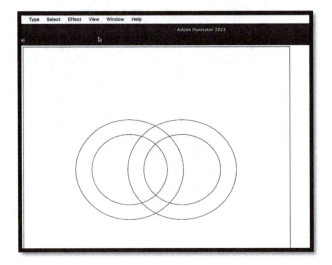

Combining shapes

Following from that you can select the Shape Builder Tool, make sure the design is selected then click and drag through segments to combine them. This is like the new intertwine feature but a bit more permanent and you can hold ALT or OPTION and click to remove segments.

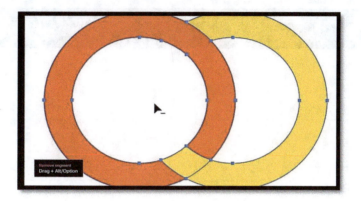

Cut a shape

Let's say you have a blue circle. Select the Scissor Tool and click anywhere on this circle to add a cut. You can now switch to the Direct Selection Tool, select a segment, and remove it and it will stop where you made that cut. Make sure you remove any duplicate anchor points and then you can grab that end Anchor Point and just wave it around.

Sample exact color with Eyedropper Tool

Next, you can use the Eyedropper Tool to copy some of the properties from one shape to another but if you'd like to sample the color (not the shapes properties), hold SHIFT and click and it will sample that exact color.

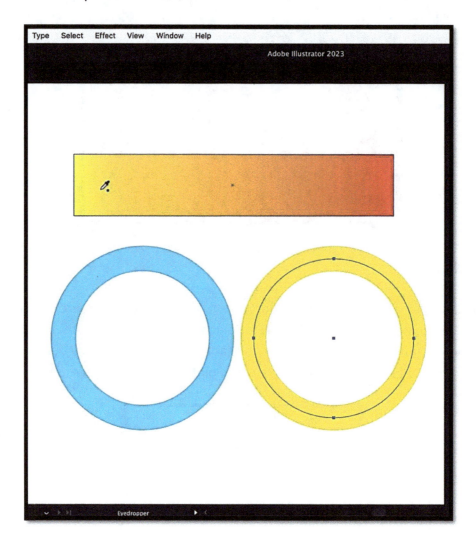

Advanced Eyedropper Tool Settings

Another quick tip: you can double-click the Eyedropper Tool and choose exactly what this tool picks up and applies.

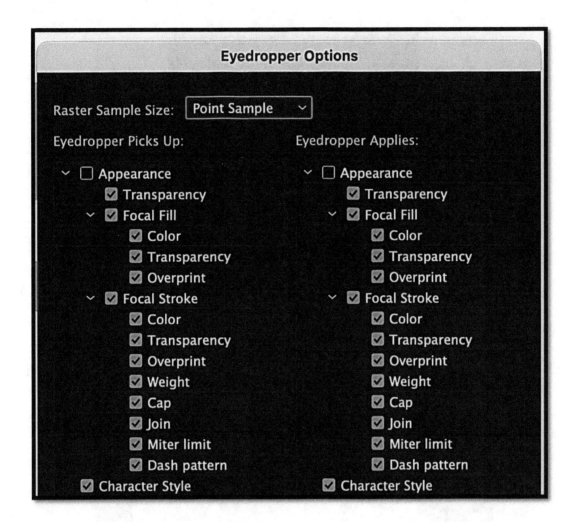

Working with arrow keys

You may know that you can adjust the properties of an object from the Transform panel using the arrow keys but did you also know you can hold down SHIFT to move in larger increments or COMMAND/CTRL to move in smaller increments?

Adjust width and height of an object

We can also use the Properties panel to adjust the width and height of an object using math. We'll simply go to the end, then go minus fifty percent, press return and the circle becomes 50% smaller. This also works for addition, multiplication, and division.

Hide grid

At some point, you will accidentally select the Perspective Tool. When you do this, something appears, and like a sane person you'll try and click the extra close; well nothing will happen and you'll enter a fit of rage. Once you eventually calm down, go to View, down to Perspective Grid and here you'll find the option to "Hide grid."

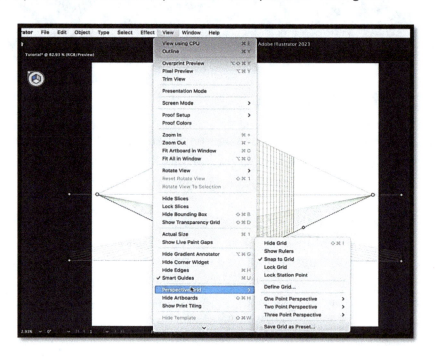

Double-clicking a group

Double-clicking a group is basically inception. You can keep double-clicking to go more layers in and a quick way out is to double-click anywhere on the workspace.

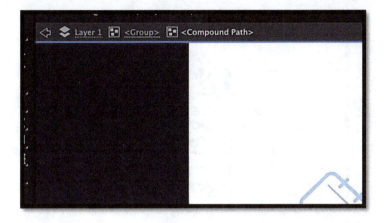

Brushes and lines

Something else you may not know is that you can go to Window then go down to Brushes, draw a line or a shape or whatever, and then from the Menu icon in the top right corner go to the Open Brush Library and choose from plenty of brushes that go with Illustrator.

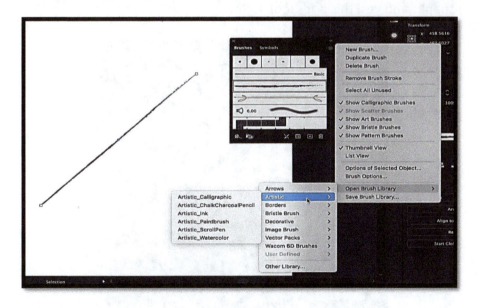

You can go for some paintbrush ones and with the line selected, you can click through and apply these different brush effects. You can also cycle through the brush categories from the bottom and you can also download and install more brush packs from other platforms.

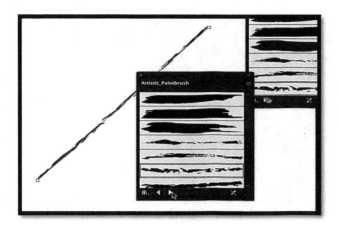

Separate intersecting shapes

We have some overlapping circles. Let's select them and select the "Divide" option from the Pathfinder panel and it will group these. So with them selected right-click and select "Ungroup" and where all of these shapes are intersecting has now been separated into individual shapes and yes, this does look right.

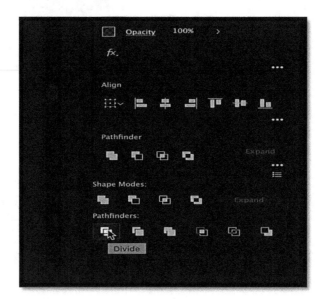

Go up to Illustrator's Preferences which is under the Edit menu if you're on Windows. Select Performance and increase "History States" to 200 so now when you screw up your design work you have the added peace of mind.

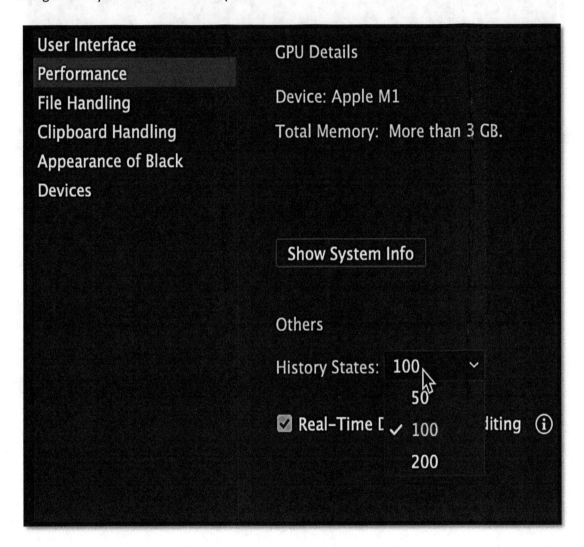

Change default location for saving files

Also, by default, Illustrator always saves to the Cloud but if you don't want that you can again go to Preferences, select "File handling" and you can now change the default location to stop this window from popping up every single time.

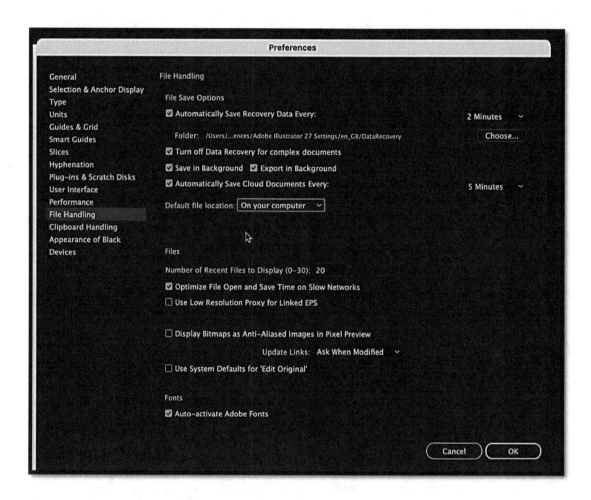

Review Questions

1. How can you intertwine overlapping shapes?
2. In what instance is a trimmed view important?
3. How can you copy appearance effects from one object to another?

INDEX

B

D

E

H

I

J

K

L

O

P

www.ingramcontent.com/pod-product-compliance
Lightning Source LLC
LaVergne TN
LVHW081519050326
832903LV00025B/1551